"*INCREDIBLE. A powerful guide filled with transformative, yet sustainable, strategies for those who desire to revolutionize the way they show up for students. A must-read for any educator who wants to make a difference.*"

—Naomi O'Brien
Educator, Public Speaker, Author

"*Wow! A professional development books that includes a fable? What a powerful and effective structure that will allow educators to feel seen and heard more than ever before. As I followed Chloe's journey, I saw flashes of my own early classroom struggles, specific student faces, and the very educator/ mentor who inducted me into our very own league of extraordinary educators. The second part of this book is beautifully paced and complete with research, experiences, and actionable steps that will induct readers as well. This was an incredibly powerful book—every educator needs this!*"

—LaNesha Tabb,
Educator, Author, Speaker

"Part 1: The Fable *is such a fun and fascinating read! It draws you in and keeps you engaged the entire time.* Part 2: The Formula *hits the nail on the pedagogical head! I believe that building positive relationships is what matters most in education, and Dr. Woodly seamlessly breaks down how to do just that, while also letting us know exactly how to be the extraordinary educators we've been called to be! Grab this one now, y'all.*"

—Dwayne Reed,
America's Favorite Rapping Teacher

"*Whether you have been in education for several years or just getting started, you will realize that the timing of this book by Dr. Shaun Woodly is very relevant today. Teachers and administrators are burned out and need tools to become extraordinary educators for their students, and this book infuses tools that work. Like Chloe, I personally loved teaching but hated it at times due to several unforeseen circumstances out of my control. This can become frustrating*

Praise for *The League of Extraordinary Educators*

"*Building upon his powerful* Teach, Hustle, Inspire *brand, Dr. Woodly has made a bold, powerful statement in his newest release where he states,* The End of Ordinary. *In these times of ongoing 'pandemic challenges,' he dug deeper in this book by sharing the strategies of extraordinary educators in culturally diverse schools. I believe strongly that if you want results, find the people who've already done it and at a high level of accomplishment. Dr. Woodly has done just that. This book promises to be a winner for all educators who read it and implement the strategies in earnest.*"

—Baruti Kafele
Education Consultant, Author, Retired Principal

"*Dr. Woodly does a fantastic job of breaking down what it means and takes to be an extraordinary educator in order to support educators in overcoming the barriers of ordinary teaching. The beginning narrative paints a picture of the many overwhelming feelings and misconceptions educators can hold and pushes against the false narratives in order to create breakthroughs. The follow up of tangible steps educators can take to create a culturally responsive learning environment where students are intrinsically motivated and feel connection to their work, peers, and teacher leading to extraordinary impacts. This book is both supportive and necessary for education today.*"

—Shane Saeed
Instructional Coach, St Vrain Valley School District

and affect your attitude and make connecting with students tough. Shane put some things in perspective for Chloe as he challenged her to change her mindset to do better by speaking to her about his shortcomings and how he overcame them to become an extraordinary educator. As Shane stated, it's time to end the ordinary and become 'Extraordinary' educators. It takes a secret society of educators to train other educators to ensure all students are given the opportunity to be successful, and this book explains how educators can better connect with their students. There is so much power in connection. Every student is one caring adult away from being a success story. If you want to be that one caring adult your students need, this book will guide you in the right direction."

—Robert Jackson
International Speaker/Award Winning ASCD Author,
Educator for 27 Years

"Shaun Woodly is a masterful storyteller who has the gift of providing fresh insight as our educational system continues to shift towards better. In The League of Extraordinary Educators: The Secret Strategies of Trans-formational Teachers, *Dr. Woodly shows us how to succeed as educators so we don't succumb to mediocrity, but more importantly create a lasting impact in our students' lives."*

—Michael Bonner
CEO of Bonnerville, 4th and 6th grade teacher at the
Ron Clark Academy, Disruptive Innovator, Entrepreneur,
Ellen Degeneres Favorite Teacher, Published Author

The League of Extraordinary Educators

The League of Extraordinary Educators

The Secret Strategies of Transformational Teachers

Shaun Woodly, PhD

JB JOSSEY-BASS™
A Wiley Brand

Library of Congress Cataloging-in-Publication Data:

Names: Woodly, Shaun, author.
Title: The league of extraordinary educators : the secret strategies of
  transformational teachers / Shaun Woodly, Ph.D.
Description: First edition. | Hoboken, New Jersey : John Wiley & Sons,
  Inc., [2023] | Includes index.
Identifiers: LCCN 2023025970 (print) | LCCN 2023025971 (ebook) | ISBN
  9781119902652 (paperback) | ISBN 9781119902669 (adobe pdf) | ISBN
  9781119902676 (epub)
Subjects: LCSH: Transformative learning—United States. | Effective
  teaching—United States. | Culturally relevant pedagogy.
Classification: LCC LC1100 .W66 2023 (print) | LCC LC1100 (ebook) | DDC
  371.1020973—dc23/eng/20230814

LC record available at https://lccn.loc.gov/2023025970
LC ebook record available at https://lccn.loc.gov/2023025971

Cover Image: © CreativeDesignArt/Getty Images
Cover Design: Wiley
Author Photo: © Mike D Shot Me LLC

SKY10056107_092523

This book is dedicated to Team Us. All of us :)

Contents

Introduction

Have you ever wondered why some teachers are able to create classrooms that radiate with energy, curiosity, and joy? Why do these teachers' students seem to be more engaged, more inspired, and more successful? That's the question that set me on a journey—a journey to discover the secret behind these extraordinary classrooms and how every teacher can create one.

I am Dr. Shaun Woodly, and I believe that teachers should enjoy the extraordinary gift of teaching and students should enjoy the extraordinary gift of learning. This belief, forged from my 15 years of experience in education—from K–12 classrooms to higher education lecture halls—has become my life's mission. As a student of this craft we call education, the experiences and insights I've gained over the years have led me to write this book. It's more than just a career for me; it's a calling. Because I believe that education can be and will be better—it will just take some time, and I have time today.

I've seen the struggles and successes of students and teachers alike in urban and culturally diverse schools. I've seen the potential for transformative education and the obstacles that can stand in its way. This book is a distillation of those experiences. It's a blueprint for creating Extraordinary classrooms and Extraordinary educators.

In the pages of this book, you'll find the tools and strategies to transform your teaching practice, to create engaging, inclusive, and innovative classrooms that inspire students and educators alike. The book is divided into two parts. The first part tells a story, because stories are the lifeblood of human culture. They are the means by which we make sense of the world around us. The story of this book is a narrative that encapsulates the journey from an ordinary to an Extraordinary educator. It's a tale that underlines the transformative power of education and the potential that lies within each student and each teacher.

The second part of the book takes you through a systematic breakdown of the formula for Extraordinary teaching. It's based on many years of research and experience, grounded in culturally responsive pedagogy, human behavior, cognitive science, educational psychology, and neuroscience. The formula is designed to guide you step by step, showing you how to create a learning environment that is rich, empowering, and transformational.

As an educator and a parent, I believe in the power to ignite the innate light within each student, to guide them in unveiling their talents, and to shine a spotlight on their unique potential. The current structure of K–12 schools insists on pushing a model that no longer suits the needs of our students. And truthfully it never did. This book is for educators who share this belief. It is for those who are ready to break free from the outdated, restrictive models of teaching that have held back students and teachers alike for far too long.

Now, you might be wondering, "What makes this book different from other educational books?" The answer lies in its unique approach. While most books focus on the "what" and "how" of teaching, this book digs deeper. It explores the "why" behind our actions and decisions, the belief systems that drive us, and the mindsets that shape our teaching practices.

Moreover, it provides a roadmap to navigate the inherent obstacles in urban and culturally diverse schools. By focusing on the power of Extraordinary Learning Experiences, Extraordinary Peer Collaboration, Extraordinary Teacher Connections, and Extraordinary Environmental Conditions, this book aims to transform ordinary classrooms into Extraordinary Learning Environments.

As someone who grew up in urban schools, taught in urban schools, researched in urban schools, and now supports teachers in urban and culturally diverse schools, I have seen and experienced this from all sides. I've seen the ordinary practices that limit what teachers and students are capable of and the extraordinary practices that release their potential.

Let's imagine a classroom where students are not just receivers of knowledge but active participants in their learning process; where their experiences, cultures, and identities are valued and integrated into the curriculum; and where teachers are not just instructors but mentors, guides, and allies. This is the extraordinary classroom that this book can help you create.

This book is a manifestation of my belief that every student can surpass the limitations imposed by a traditional, or better yet "ordinary," education system. It's a testament to my conviction that every educator has the power to transform their classroom. It's an invitation for you to join me in this movement, to create a ripple effect of change that will resonate across classrooms, schools, and communities in this nation and beyond.

Education is a journey, not a destination. It's a process of continuous growth, exploration, and transformation. And this journey becomes extraordinary when we, as educators, are willing to go beyond the ordinary, to challenge ourselves, to strive for excellence, and to inspire our students to do the same.

We can do better. We *must* do better. For our students, for our communities, for our future. This book is my contribution to that effort, a guide to help you join the movement of Extraordinary educators transforming the world, one classroom at a time. Let's end ordinary. Let's become extraordinary.

I

The Fable

The Scenario

Chloe Yearwood really loves teaching, but she is starting to hate being a teacher. The profession she has put so much into, the profession she studied so hard for, the profession she has given so much to, it isn't giving anything in return but stress and endless problems.

If it isn't complaining parents, it is pressure for standardized test performance. If it isn't students who can't seem to retain anything taught, it is them being outright disrespectful, always talking back or worse.

In her apartment, she begins to prepare for her day. A small space is filled with remnants of her profession. Stacks of textbooks teeter on the edge of her worn-out couch, a multitude of colorful stationery is littered across her coffee table, and a whiteboard with half-erased notes and reminders leans against the wall. On her table is a mountain of papers she has yet to grade, each representing a student, a young mind she is responsible for shaping. It is a space that screams "educator," just as much as it whispers "exhaustion."

Chloe is the youngest of three, her parents having her older brother Clark when they were just starting their lives together. There is a 15-year gap between her and Clark, and although they share the same parents, they seem to share very little else. Chloe has always been closer to her sister Camille, who is three years older than her. They were thick as thieves growing up, their bond only strengthening after the death of their parents when Chloe was 10.

Chloe's father was the town's beloved plumber, a self-made man whose work ethic was only surpassed by his desire to help others. Her mother was a pillar in the community, a well-respected educator who had instilled in Chloe a deep love for teaching, a very genuine and kind-hearted woman who fiercely advocated for better education and learning experiences for all children. She believed with every bit of her character that it is possible, for both teachers and students, to create a world where every day feels like the first day of school. She believed it is possible for education to be a place of excitement, enthusiasm, and joy. She believed it is possible for education to be a place where, regardless of what is going on in the outside world, the four walls of a classroom can be a place where every and any child can feel valued, be safe, and know that they are welcome.

But the shadow of her brother Clark loomed greatly over their family. Clark was always "different." He struggled in school, socially and academically, and holds a deep-seated resentment toward his parents. Where Chloe saw her parents' advocacy and passion for education as inspiring, Clark saw it as suffocating. He was a specter in their lives, and as he got older, his disconnection from the family was always a source of silent tension.

With the death of their parents, Clark seemed to disappear completely, his presence replaced by a void that Chloe and Camille could only fill with each other. They were raised by an aunt and uncle, the structure of their small family forever altered, the absence of their brother a constant, silent companion.

Chloe is now 31 years old and on the brink of questioning everything. She is a teacher, a role she had taken on proudly, doing her best to carry on the legacy of her mother. But lately, she feels the passion waning, replaced by a rising tide of frustration and burnout. The policies and politics, the testing, the students' lack of respect, the constant battle to stay afloat, it is all starting to take its toll.

Just yesterday, in a really tense moment, she had to catch herself from escalating a situation with a student that could have been so much worse. Chloe walked down the row of desks, handing each student back their quizzes while explaining that she expected so much more from her students. She walked by her student Mya, holding the paper upside down and slightly folded as to exercise some discretion with the grade that would soon be discovered. Mya already knew what that signal was and simultaneously sucked her teeth, snatched the paper out of Chloe's hand, and mumbled something she didn't care if her teacher heard or not.

Almost immediately, Chloe raised one eyebrow and shot a scathing look at the student that would have pierced through a brick wall. In a matter of a half a second, several choice words flooded Chloe's thoughts, and she was fully prepared to give Mya a piece of her mind, and more, and deliver an epic clap-back. Chloe was prepared to choose violence. But, although that student chose to go low, Chloe chose to go high and to say to herself, "She's just a child. She's just a child" as she made the job-saving choice to move on and finish handing out the remaining grades.

Every time she seems to take one step forward with her students, they always seem to take two steps back. She has been teaching for 5 years and truly thinks she is in the classroom to live out her calling. But almost every day she feels like she is fighting just to stay afloat.

On the way out of the door, her gaze falls on an old photograph, a faded memory of her family. Chloe, just a toddler, Camille with a gap-toothed smile, Clark with his arms crossed and a look that was unresponsive, their parents beaming at the camera.

Illumination Academy

Illumination Academy, where Chloe teaches, has its share of challenges and those challenges are evident in her classroom. Her students are all over the place academically. Some are on grade level, some above, and more are below. She knows her content forward and backward but regularly struggles to keep the students' attention for any length of time. Their attitude toward school and desire to learn seems nonexistent. Although she keeps trying, her resilience is fleeting.

Although Illumination Academy has its struggles, it wasn't always like this. Upon the doors first opening more than 70 years ago, the school was christened Grady Heights School of the Arts. But that name didn't seem to resonate with the vision of the community or the vibrant spirit of its students. The school was swarming with young minds ablaze with curiosity and creativity, their potential twinkling like distant stars. It was clear that the name "Grady Heights School of the Arts" fell short in capturing the sheer brilliance of these young minds.

Just a few months after its doors opened, with a unanimous decision by the school board and the support of the community, a transformative decision was made. The school was renamed "Illumination Academy," a name that better embodied the vibrance and promise of its students. The new name was a reflection of the school's mission—to ignite the innate light within each student, to guide them in unveiling their talents, and to shine a spotlight on their unique potential.

The school board deeply believed in the boundless capability of its students. They believed that each child held within them a radiant light—a brilliant blend of talents, passions, and potential. They saw it as their duty to nurture this light, allowing it to grow brighter with each passing day. Thus, Illumination Academy became more than just a name. It became a beacon of hope for the community, a testament to the belief in the boundless potential of each child. The teachers saw themselves as "illuminators," aiding in the discovery and development of the inherent brightness within each student.

In its early days, Illumination Academy played host to some of the brightest minds in Grady Heights. Nestled in the heart of the community, teachers would often walk to work, and parents could often be found volunteering their time and talents toward the upkeep of the building. Illumination Academy was more than just a school; it was the very cornerstone of the community. Neighborhood events became a tradition at the school, drawing together everyone in the spirit of connection and camaraderie, reinforcing the school's pivotal role in the social fabric of the community.

However, despite its storied past and rich heritage, changing times and a corrupt organization brought a string of challenges that saw the academy's once-shining reputation begin to dim. Oppressive education policies and outdated practices started to undermine the once-thriving intellectual environment. The emphasis on standardized testing and the insistent use of one-size-fits-all teaching methods began to replace the creative and tailored approaches that the academy was known for, leaving students disengaged, unenthused, and achieving at extremely low levels.

This went on for decades, the consequences of which inevitably spread outside the school walls into the community. Grady Heights became marred with poverty and struggle. Once known for its abundance of intellectual treasure, the narrative surrounding Grady Heights changed drastically.

What a Day

Chloe closes the door behind herself after escorting her students to their buses. She needs to sit down for a few minutes to breathe. Her legs practically give out, and she falls back into her chair with enough force to fall through the floor. Some days are better than others, and she is doing the best she can. But doggone it if it isn't starting to wear her out. For Chloe Yearwood it feels like she has given everything she has for the week, and it is only Tuesday.

Day by day, her love for children and the art of what it means to be a teacher dwindle more and more. She wonders if this is truly where she is supposed to be. Should she have been an accountant instead? Perhaps it's time to explore those office jobs all of her other friends have. She shudders at the thought, but she is beginning to feel like she has no choice. Education is wearing her out, and she just isn't sure how much more she can take.

As she ruminates, Chloe's colleague and teacher-bestie Ian steps into the room for their normal after-work chat. But today, there isn't much talking. Ian plops down on a chair in front of Chloe. He stretches out his legs, throws his head back, and palms his forehead. After a moment or two, Ian sits up and looks at Chloe. They exchange a glance that says, "This has been a day!" without saying a word.

Chloe and Ian became good friends teaching the same grade level last year. Being a part of the same professional learning community in the building gives them plenty of opportunities to work together. Between sharing their teacher stories, planning lessons, and even the occasional side-eye at someone else that evolved into an inside joke, it did not take long for them to become good friends.

"These kids were on one today," Ian says breaking the restful silence.

Smiling through her fatigue, "Little Ms. Mya Anderson almost made me lose my job today. I was *this* close to giving her a piece of my mind," Chloe says as she brings her thumb and index finger together within a hairline distance of one another.

Ian chuckles as he sits up, nodding in agreement with Chloe. "She get upset about her grade again?"

Chloe nods.

"I swear I don't know what it is. I stand in front of my class daily and teach the lessons, many more than once. And it never fails—they're either distracted by something or looking at me like I have two heads. The ones who do pay attention, the information goes in one ear and out the other!" Ian exclaims.

Instinctively Chloe looks up at the clock in her classroom just as the announcement is made: "All faculty and staff members please report to the media center for our faculty meeting. All faculty and staff members please report to the media center for our faculty meeting."

Ian and Chloe look at each other as if to say, "Let's just go ahead and get this over with." They both reluctantly get up and shuffle toward the door. Just as the door is about to close, Chloe darts back into the room with a quick surge of energy. Her desk drawer flies open as she rummages through her stash for a candy bar.

"I deserve this," she says, smiling while looking at a mini Snickers bar. "We both do." Chloe tosses a second one to Ian. "Okay, now we can go." Those candy bars are gone before they even make it to the media center.

The Faculty Meeting

In the faculty meeting, Chloe is there physically, but mentally she has decided to check out for the day. She is there for one reason and one reason only—because she has to be. After the day she had, she wants nothing more than to get out of that building as fast as possible, but missing monthly faculty meetings is not an option. So she is there, but at the same time she isn't.

The clapping brings Chloe out of her daze just long enough to see her colleague, Shane, is being recognized for his students' academic success. After making his way to the front, Shane accepts the honor with a bright smile as he shakes hands with the principal.

Shane is clearly a rising rock star at Illumination Academy. This makes the third consecutive month that Shane's students have showed the highest academic gains. And these are not small gains either. All of his students—the ones on, at, and below grade level—are making significant gains, and it is something truly to be commended. And this comes after another colleague, April, had been recognized two consecutive times before. What is it that they are doing that got them such good results on a consistent basis?

The meeting finally adjourns, and Chloe can only hope she didn't miss anything super important. Besides seeing Shane accept his certificate, the rest of the meeting is a blur. Chloe makes her way through the funnel of teachers to get out of the media center. Out of the corner of her eye she sees the award-winning teacher and darts in his direction.

Shane pushes in his chair as he begins to make his way out of the media center. He has his certificate in one hand and his bag draped over his shoulder as Chloe walks up to him.

"Congratulations, Shane," Chloe says with a smile. "I can barely get my students to focus, and you're breaking world records." She says jokingly, "You must truly be doing some magical things in that classroom."

Humbly, but with an air of confidence, Shane replies, "We make some things happen in there. I wouldn't say it's magic—more like, science."

The response puzzles Chloe a bit, and she isn't quite sure how to respond. What does he mean by that? And more importantly, how the heck is he able to have so much success when Chloe is struggling?

Shane is someone who Chloe sees often in passing. Often very polite and cordial, Shane will occasionally say, "Hello" or "Have a good one," accompanied with a smile, but always seems to be on his way somewhere important. Anytime Chloe sees him with anyone, it is always the same two people: Ethan and April.

Chloe also notices something else about the three of them. They each wear very distinct glasses and a pin. It isn't terribly obvious, but it caught her eye one day. Chloe had just left the teachers' lounge after having lunch and was making her way back to her classroom. In the hallway, she could hear the laughter coming from April's classroom. Chloe likes a good joke and wanted to see what there was to laugh about too. Offering a welcoming smile, she peeked her head in the room to see Shane, Ethan, and April engaged in a conversation that seemed to be pretty funny.

Noticing Chloe, they seemed to all of a sudden need to finish the conversation at another time. "Let me go get my students from the cafeteria. I'll talk to you guys later," Shane had said as he made his way to the door, still laughing a bit. "Hey, Chloe," he had said with a smile.

Chloe caught a glimpse of the pin on the lapel of his blazer as Shane made his way out of the door. Although she couldn't really tell what the pin said, she couldn't help but notice it because the shiny gold twinkled under the fluorescent classroom lights as if it had just been polished. Several times after that she noticed this same pin but didn't think much about it because it was just that. A simple pin. It isn't until today that she notices Ethan and April seem to have the same pin with the same glasses. And it is just those three. No one else.

Having the opportunity to speak with Shane after the faculty meeting, she now sees the pin up close. She examines it to discover it reads "Teach Hustle Inspire." Small, but shiny and bright. Not a fingerprint on it, and it lay perfectly straight as if placed with a T-square. Curious, she asks, "That's a nice pin. Where'd you get it?"

Looking down at it then looking back at Chloe, Shane smiles and replies, "I earned it."

Guidance

Smiling but also furrowing her brow, she is a bit confused at Shane's response. Not thinking too much about it in the moment, Chloe says, "Congratulations on your students' success!"

"Thanks! It wasn't easy, especially coming off the heels of April and Ethan doing so well too. It's not a contest, but does often become a little friendly competition among us to see how our students match up each month. At the end of the day, as long as our kids are improving, we're happy," Shane says as he looks back at the other two, April smiling while cleaning the lens of her glasses.

"Looks like the three of you got lucky. I can barely get mine to pay attention long enough to get through a lesson, let alone perform well. Unless there are Starbursts involved," Chloe says, laughing.

Shane offers a smile and empty giggle. He didn't find what Chloe said particularly funny but he also doesn't want to be rude.

Sensing a bit of the awkwardness, she quickly continues, "So, what's really going on in your classroom? Three consecutive months of significant student gains. That's some incredible luck!"

Adjusting his coat, Shane takes the opportunity to gently push back. "It's not luck, please believe that," he offers with a smile.

"Well, maybe you can work some of that magic on my students," Chloe says jokingly. "Yes, teach me your ways," she says to the trio as she lifts her hands in the air in a playfully mocking, but also partially serious manner.

"I'd be happy to," Shane says matter-of-factly.

Chloe is surprised but also replies, "Seriously?"

Shane looks back at Ethan and April and shrugs. He turns back to Chloe. "Why not? How about sometime this week I stop by your room and sit in on a lesson or two? You know, just to check things out?"

Although Chloe definitely isn't prepared for or expecting this transaction to take place on the backend of a faculty meeting, she is a little excited. If she could get ahold of just half of the strategies in Shane's classroom, what a difference that would make. A sense of relief washes over her. She begins to get hopeful about the future and what that could mean for her as well as her students.

"That'd be great," Chloe says with a smile.

"Good, I'll speak to Principal Williams to see about getting sub coverage Thursday for my class so that I can sit in on yours. Cool?"

"Cool," Chloe says.

Shane smiles, "It's settled."

He extends his hand. As Chloe takes his hand to seal the deal he says, "Hi, my name is Shane, and I'm your Connection Mentor."

An Emergency Meeting

Chloe walks into the building the next morning only to be greeted at the door by a sign. It reads, "Emergency faculty meeting this morning. Please report to the media center immediately." Chloe thinks that is extremely odd as they just had their regular meeting yesterday afternoon. As she makes her way into the space, there is a whirlwind of whispers, hurried shuffling of papers, and the clinking of mugs as teachers gather for the emergency staff meeting. The air buzzes with a mix of apprehension and curiosity. These types of meetings are only one of two things—something really good or something really bad. Considering the awards given out just the day before, everyone begins to sense it is the latter. Principal Williams stands at the front of the room, her eyes sweeping over the gathered educators. She is a tall figure, the lines on her face reflecting years of service dedicated to education and the institution she now leads. The room grows silent as she clears her throat.

"Good morning, everyone," she begins, her voice steady despite the inferred gravity of the situation. The silent room seems to swallow her words. "I won't beat around the bush. We're in trouble. A lot of trouble."

A hush falls over the room, the weight of her words settling like a heavy fog. Her gaze meets the eyes of the teachers—dedicated educators who have given their best to the academy and its students.

"Test scores," she continues, letting the words hang in the air, "have been falling steadily for years. Despite our best efforts, despite our dedication and commitment, we are failing to meet the standards set by the state."

A murmur runs through the room, the sound of shifting chairs and uneasy sighs filling the air.

"And if we don't act now, if we don't find a way to turn things around, our beloved academy risks closure," she finishes, her voice barely more than a whisper at this point.

A stunned silence follows. The once vibrant room is filled with a sense of disbelief, faces reflecting a mix of shock, concern, and a quiet resolve. The threat of closure has been whispered in hushed tones before, but hearing it confirmed aloud is a jarring reality check.

Principal Williams looks at them all, her gaze steady and unyielding. "This is our last chance. If we don't see a total change in our spring achievement data, this could be it for us. We have a choice," she says, voice firm now, her words slicing through the silence. "We can let this be the end of our journey, or we can fight."

After the meeting, Chloe doesn't really know what to think. She sits there for a moment before realizing she still has to get ready for the day and begin class soon. Students are starting to make their way into the building.

Chloe's Classroom

Chloe walks into the classroom to find Shane already there. "That was pretty heavy, huh?" he says. Chloe nods in agreement. No sooner do they finish the exchange than students begin to walk into the room. Holding any further conversation until later, Shane signals to Chloe, "We'll talk later."

Chloe puts her bags and coat down as the student chatter begins to ring through the air. She's not entirely sure if she's ready for the day's instruction. The students enter the classroom—some go hang up their coats, others gather around and chat with friends, while a select few just quietly take their seats. In no time, the morning announcements begin over the loudspeaker but can barely be heard. Chloe calls out to the students, "Excuse me, the announcements are on!"

"Sorry, Ms. Yearwood," she hears a student call. The rest respond by finishing up their conversations, shuffling their way to their desks, only to have missed everything that the principal said.

Shane makes some observations. Her teaching style is centered in whole-class instruction. It is not hard to tell that she is very comfortable here. She teaches with lectures, often standing in front of the class to present subject matter. She facilitates discussions among the students and does her best to get students to actively participate.

Typically, as she begins she has the students' attention, but it isn't long before she finds herself issuing calls for them to stay focused in almost every lesson. Chloe writes a few things on the board with the expectation that the students do the same on their worksheets. The notes on the board often don't make it to the worksheets, however. Doodles and sketches often find their way into the students' notes instead, if anything at all.

It almost never fails; the hand of a student will make its way to the air accompanied by a puzzled look.

"Ms. Yearwood, what do we need to know this for?" the student asks with all sincerity.

"It's on the test," Chloe replies, with the expectation that her answer will be all the student needs to regain focus, put forth his or her best effort, and stay engaged during instruction. Chloe, clearly frustrated, sees that students are not engaged the way she needs them to be. She finds herself spending a lot of time and energy trying to motivate them. She has a solid collection of candy she keeps on hand, and she has even set up a bulletin board to reward students for their achievements. Regardless, everything she tries still ends up with students who barely engage, some who comply just to avoid getting in trouble, and others who just downright choose to do other things in the middle of class. This type of apathy, defiance, and low morale keeps Chloe in a constant state of frustration and exhaustion.

Chloe typically assigns homework based on the day's discussions with the intent that students review their notes, complete the assignment, and prepare for upcoming quizzes and tests.

Walking up and down the desk rows, Chloe offers directions to her students. "This worksheet that I'm handing to you, I expect this to be done today, and we'll go over it tomor . . ." Her instructions to the class are suddenly interrupted as she tries to regain her balance from stumbling over a student's book bag. This book bag, a familiar bright pink book bag with black stripes, almost causes Chloe to trip in what could have been a very embarrassing moment for her. She shoots a look at a nearby student.

"Mya, what is your bag doing in the middle of the aisle again, when it should be on your hook like everybody else's?"

Mya attempts to plead with Chloe, claiming that she needs her book bag nearby. Chloe isn't having it, and with some stern threats makes Mya hang up her book bag.

Shane sits toward the back of the room, quietly taking everything in without judgment, but Chloe feels judgment anyway.

The Day Is Finally Over

Shane helps Chloe as she begins to wrap up the day. He takes the time to assist her in getting her students packed up, make sure they line up at the door, and walk toward the buses and parent pickup area as efficiently as possible.

They make their way back to Chloe's room to debrief the day. Without being prompted, Chloe goes right into an explanation of the day's events.

"I tell you these kids are something else. It's like pulling teeth trying to get them to pay attention. I had to explain some of the concepts like three or four times today, did you see that? They need to do a better job focusing, or they're going to find themselves right back here next year!"

Shane just nods. Chloe continues.

"I know you haven't been here at Illumination Academy long, but the community the students live in has its. . .concerns, I'll just say."

Chloe begins to walk toward the window and goes to a familiar place in her mind.

"You know. . . since before I can remember I wanted to be a teacher. When I was younger I would teach my students, my Cabbage Patch Kids and Barbie Dolls. I taught the absolute best lessons, teaching them about outer space and how to properly add 2 + 2. I made sure everyone was paying attention to the valuable lessons taught; otherwise, they would have detention. But detention was rarely the case because my students were perfect. Perfect listeners, perfect learners, and perfect pupils. And I was the perfect teacher."

"It's funny," she continues. "When I was in high school, my teachers would tell me 'You'll make a great teacher one day.' I'd smile every time because I truly believed I would be a great teacher. I mean I studied education in college, sailed through my courses, and couldn't wait to start my student teaching experience. I even got lucky enough to be placed at a school that reminded me so much of the school I attended as a student. I had so many great experiences as a student, and I wanted to offer that same love for learning to the students I taught."

"Although I enjoyed being a student teacher, I couldn't wait until I had a classroom of my own. When getting ready for graduation, I started submitting applications for teaching positions. I tried as much as I could to stay close to home, but the availability just wasn't there. I searched and searched, this time going a little bit farther away from home. I was ready to step into my calling and if that meant I had to go a little farther away then so be it. I got this position at Illumination Academy and was very excited, but I have to say this is not what I'm used to."

Shane just sits back and listens with an empathic ear.

Turning back toward Shane, Chloe continues with an elevated level of frustration in her tone. "It just seems like I always get the short end of the stick. I always get the struggling learners who are one, two, sometimes even three grade levels behind. Even for my students who are supposedly on grade level, it's a constant battle to get them to focus and do what they are supposed to do. Like today, I literally had to go over some parts of the lesson multiple times."

Shane just listens without judgment, even though Chloe still feels like she is on trial. At the root of Chloe's excuses, she truly believes the group of students she has are different than Shane's and she needs to give context as to why engagement is so low.

"Chloe," Shane says, "I understand everything that you're saying; trust me, I deal with the same thing."

Chloe clearly does not believe him.

"Let me ask you a question," Shane says. "You say your students struggle to stay engaged. But what reason do they have to stay engaged?"

Chloe's feelings of embarrassment begin to shift to criticism because she doesn't like where this is going and it shows on her face.

"I'm the teacher! I'm giving everything I have to set my students up for success. The least they can do is pay attention," she fires back.

"You mean just like you were paying attention in the faculty meeting yesterday?" Shane interjects.

Chloe wasn't expecting that. She thought for a second and tries to find the best words to convey that it's not the same thing, but Shane continues.

"Look, I am not here to judge. I'm on your side and want to help. I have an idea. Tomorrow, why don't you sit in on my class while your kids are in P.E. and I'll show you what I mean."

Chloe raises an eyebrow as she thinks for a few seconds. "Just for a few minutes, stop by, and I'll explain everything," he encourages.

A Whole New World

Chloe walks into Shane's room after walking her students to P.E. She usually likes to take this time to sit in her classroom and decompress or chat with Ian about the goings-on of anything other than school to take her mind off teaching for a few moments. Although she would have preferred to enjoy her usual time of peace, she figures she would oblige Shane's request to step into his classroom and see what is going on.

She looks around and can't help but notice the commotion. They are clearly in the middle of something, but she can't move past the fact that the desks are not in straight rows and students are up and out of their seats. It isn't chaotic, but it certainly isn't what Chloe is used to.

Shane, sitting at a kidney-shaped desk with a group of students, looks up and smiles at Chloe to acknowledge her presence. "Ms. Yearwood, hello! Feel free to walk around if you'd like. Let me know if you have any questions." He brings his attention back to the small group of students at his table.

Chloe cautiously and curiously walks around Shane's room. Although a bit noisier than she is used to, she can't help but notice the sense of enthusiasm among the students. The only time she's felt that level of excitement in her room is when the students are getting ready for a field trip. She wonders if they are getting ready to leave at some point soon.

One student is addressing the others in her group: "Here, you take this and add it to this cup. Once you do that, go ahead and mix it up. While he's doing that, take a look at the results and write it down so we can see if it changes."

"What are you all up to?" Chloe asks the student who seems to be in charge.

"Hi, Ms. Yearwood! At this station, we're mixing different things to see if they're heterogeneous or homogenous." Pointing to each of the participants, she continues, "She gathers the materials and makes sure we have everything. He does the mixing, she writes everything down, and I'm responsible for making sure it all gets done."

"Wow," Chloe says to the student. "Thanks for telling me. You all keep up the good work."

It is interesting to Chloe because, even though Shane's room is just three doors down, the air in there just feels different. There isn't as much tension as there is in Chloe's room, and although it is a bit on the noisy side, it isn't hard to tell there is a level of focus and engagement that she hasn't seen before.

A loud "What are you doing!" comes from across the room. It immediately catches Chloe's attention because it is an all too familiar voice: Randell Carter, one of the notorious Carter brothers who Chloe had just last year. Almost every teacher is aware of these three students. A lot of the teachers struggle with them, and because of their ages, it seems like every time one left to go to the next school, another was right behind him to cause just as much trouble.

Randell Carter drove Chloe to levels of frustration she didn't think she could get to last year. No matter what she did, no matter what she said, Randell always had something to say back to her. He is the type of student who has no filter and bosses other students around as his way of expressing himself.

Shane, noticing this can potentially escalate, walks over to the group with Randell. All he does is look at Randell.

"She's not doing what I asked," Randell says, pleading his case. Shane listens, maintaining direct eye contact with Randell. Shane understands what it is that Randell really wants.

Very sternly and directly, Shane addresses Randell, "You've done well staying on task. Don't let all of your hard work go out of the window by losing control. Do you understand?"

Randell nods his head. Shane then turns to one of Randell's group members who has a puzzled look on her face. What Shane did next really throws Chloe for a loop. As he starts helping this student understand the ideas of heterogeneous and homogenous mixtures, his volume, voice inflection, and tonality shift in the blink of an eye. It is like he becomes a totally different person.

The light bulb switches on as the student says, "Ohhhh, I get it now!" and she smiles. Shane pats her on the back and encourages the group to keep going as he makes his way back to the group of students he was working with.

A few moments later, the timer goes off. Almost instantly, the students spring into action. In each group, certain students collect the materials, others gather papers to turn in, some reorganize the desks, and the remaining check for any lingering debris on the floor to make sure everything is spotless. It is like a well-oiled machine.

Chloe realizes this transition means it is time for her to collect her students.

"That 40 minutes went by fast," she says out loud looking at her watch. As she begins to head out of the door, she shoots a look to Shane as if to say thanks. Shane nods and smiles again as he continues to help his students clean up and collect their science work.

It's on the Test

Shane walks into Chloe's room as she is getting herself ready to go home.

"Amazing class," Chloe says. "You definitely got dealt a lucky hand this year. And how you got little Randell Carter to engage is beyond me." She laughs as she puts on her coat. "Let's trade rosters," Chloe says jokingly.

"Poverty. Single parent homes. Reading below grade level. Chronic behavior concerns," Shane says cutting through the laughter. "These are all of the concerns that were brought to me about my students. They deal with the same exact issues yours do."

Still not convinced, Chloe claims, "Well, you're clearly a natural."

Feeling offended at the lack of recognition of his hard work, Shane bites his tongue, holding back on his initial response. He instead says, "No, not a natural at all. Actually, I had some very humble beginnings." He goes on to explain, "I was not a very good teacher. As a matter of fact, the only thing I was good at was teaching the same way I was taught. In an ordinary way, getting ordinary results."

"Well, clearly those techniques worked in some way. I mean, you're here, which means you graduated from school," Chloe says.

"Yes, as an adult I now recognize I was fortunate enough to have the resilience it took to 'make it through,' but that just means I succeeded in spite of, not because of," Shane clarifies. "Let me ask you something. What is your role as a teacher?"

Chloe looks confused. Shane continues, "I'm asking, as an educator, what do you do? Like, how is it that you see yourself?"

Chloe cautiously begins to explain, "Well, I teach my students the curriculum and do the best I can to manage behavior while doing so."

"What do you mean?" Shane probes as Chloe gives Shane a side-eye, truly confused about this line of questioning. "How about this. What's the goal when you plan learning activities for your students? Like, what reason do *you* give students to put their energy toward what you're trying to teach?"

Now Chloe is really confused. "Because they have to know what I'm teaching them. It's on the test."

Shane continues, "While you and I both know the benefits of a solid education and the outcomes that exist on the other side of their efforts in the classroom, unfortunately, the rationale of 'because it's on the test' is not enough of a reason for students to invest their time and attention while in the learning environment."

Looking at Chloe, Shane goes on, "Haven't you noticed how much energy we put into trying to get students to focus, be on time, and try harder?"

"Heck yeah," Chloe exclaims.

"This effort is always one-sided, and there's a simple explanation for that. There's nothing in it for them," Shane concludes.

A bit confused, Chloe interjects, "Um, I don't know if I agree. I'd say my class is successful! The ones that put in the effort get the results."

Shane raises an eyebrow. "So how many 'put in the effort'?" he asks, using his fingers as air quotes.

"Almost half," Chloe responds matter-of-factly.

"So you're happy with half your class being successful? What about the rest of those children?" Shane inquires.

"They need to try harder," Chloe replies.

"Do they need to try harder or do you need to try harder?" Shane asks.

Chloe is a bit taken aback, her facial expression clearly saying, "Did he really just say that?"

"Listen," she says as she composes herself. "I tell them every single time: they need to do their best because if they don't try, it'll show up in their grade. Everything we learn in class is on the test!"

"Chloe, trust me, I hear you, and I understand. I used to tell my students the same exact thing. And you know what it got me? The same exact thing you have. Low levels of student achievement and high levels of frustration. What I had to learn is that 'it's on the test' is not a strong enough motivator for students. It doesn't mean they're incapable; it just means I was not creating the right conditions for my students to be successful.

"You have to understand; there's a lot at stake here. And I'm not just talking about grades. Like, have you noticed one of your students collects food from the cafeteria to bring home to her family?"

Chloe, stunned, looks at Shane with confusion.

"Yes," he replies. "Your student Mya. She volunteers almost every day to help the custodians clean up the cafeteria after lunch. When she thinks no one is looking, she quickly stuffs milk, leftover chicken nuggets, and fruit cups right in her book bag. The pink one with black stripes."

Chloe, truly in shock, doesn't know what to say.

"It's not hard to see that her family has fallen on tough times," Shane continues. "Right now, she has the responsibility to bring food home so that her family has enough to eat. What you have to realize is, when we do not teach our students, truly unlocking their intellectual treasure, all we do is perpetuate this cycle. Some students, yes, they have the talent and abilities, some have the grit to overcome obstacles and motivate themselves, but what about the rest? They need you! Or else, they end up one of the millions of students who drop out every year. No education; no way to earn a good living. They end up living in poverty, in jail, or worse. Again, you have to understand, a lot is at stake.

"What tends to be the unfortunate circumstance, especially for schools like ours in urban communities, is that many students are simply not achieving at high levels. Meaning they are not developing the knowledge, skills, and confidence they need to succeed in school and life beyond school. They are not developing the critical thinking and problem-solving skills, which are essential for success in today's rapidly changing world."

"I hear you," Chloe replies. "But these students are so easily distracted, always complaining, and have little to no persistence when challenges arise. I don't know, I worry that these students just don't seem to have the discipline it takes to be successful academically," Chloe says defensively.

"Okay," Shane says in agreement with her. "And when your students struggle with the material, how do you respond?"

"I reteach the lessons, but eventually at some point I have to move on, so I do," Chloe says.

"I'm just trying to help you see," Shane replies. "You're legitimately expecting new and exciting displays of student growth and transformation, using the same ordinary style and techniques you've always used.

"What you have to understand, especially for traditionally underserved and low-income communities, is that it takes extraordinary instruction to help children break out of the cycle of underachievement. When these students are prepared with extraordinary learning experiences, they are more likely to also have better health outcomes, higher levels of self-esteem, and vital social skills. They are also more likely to be engaged in their communities and to have a sense of purpose and direction in life. The positive benefits of a solid education are endless. There's too much at stake for us to be just ordinary."

An Ordinary Teacher

Shane realizes that Chloe is clearly overwhelmed, so he changes his approach.

"Look," explains Shane, "I was just like you—an ordinary teacher. I did not get my first teaching position in the usual fashion. It was 6 weeks into the school year, and I hadn't landed anything yet. I'd been searching for so long, but it seemed like no matter where I looked, there wasn't anything available. I decided to expand my search a little, as previously I was only looking in the two neighboring districts. I decided to extend my search, and if anything came of it, there'd definitely be more travel involved, but I knew it would be worth it.

"I was teaching at a school in an urban community, and the schools in this district varied from building to building. Depending on the part of town, there were big differences in the buildings, resources, and student demographics. Because of where we were, we didn't have the new building, the 1:1 student to laptop ratio, or anything close to it.

"The first thing I did in this expanded search was call the central office to see if anything was available. Now, this is by far not a normal practice, as all positions are normally posted online. You submit your application, wait for a call back, and hopefully schedule an interview. But not me. Nope, I had to be different. And what do you know, the nice young lady answered the phone and told me that something had just opened up. I couldn't believe it. I had my shot, and I was going to make the best of it. The human resources rep I spoke with told me to send along my information, and she would forward it to the building principal, who would then schedule an interview. Not 24 hours later, my phone was ringing, and the interview was scheduled—Thursday morning, 11:00 a.m.

"At this point in the year, I came in 6 weeks into the school year. I had to make up for lost time. I had to show them who was boss. I had to let them know I am not the one. I had walked into a situation where just 2 weeks earlier, the teacher had quit after less than a month on the job. That right there told me the students I was to teach were going to be a challenge. But I refused to let that deter me. I was going to walk in there, show them who was boss, and get this thing back on track. All that being said, here's what I concluded: the school was in an urban area, the students had run the previous teacher out of the building, and we were already 6 weeks into the school, so I had no time to waste.

"My early days teaching in an urban school, I wanted to convey the message that I was about business and there were no games being played in my classroom. Zero!"

Chloe likes the sound of that and hoped he would get into the big secret as to how he became such a great educator.

Shane continues, "From the first day I walked into that building, I was buttoned up in a suit, tie, shined shoes, and a firm attitude on this thing called teaching. I knew that I wanted respect, and I knew that at the age of 22 I had to demand it from day 1. And that is what I did. What I did not realize was the narrative I'd told myself created a paradigm that would severely limit my success early in my career.

"So when I walked into that classroom, having already decided what kind of students I was dealing with based on everything but my interactions with the actual students, I had cemented what it was I thought about those students and refused to budge. Every day for my first 2 years of teaching, I wore a suit and a firm attitude. I did not smile very much. I often raised my voice and would on occasion use sarcasm as a form of discipline."

Chloe's initial thought is, "What's so bad about that?"

"I was a teacher who was very cold, disconnected, and transactional," Shane continues. "I did not present myself as someone the students wanted to connect to, nor was I truly interested in connecting with them. For me, I was an ordinary educator, teaching ordinary lessons in an ordinary way. And I hated it. And, although you may not be taking the same stern approach I did, if I'm being honest, it looks like you're starting to hate this too."

As Chloe sits there, she realizes that Shane is right. So many thoughts swirl in her head. On one hand, she feels a bit of relief because she feels like Shane really understands her challenges. On the other, this feeling of confusion begins to settle in her mind because she isn't truly sure what to do about it. Shane has to have some answers, Chloe thinks, because he clearly is not that kind of teacher anymore.

"Then how did you do it?" Chloe asks. "How did you start like that, but end up like this?"

"A mentor," he says simply. "A teacher that saw through my facade, saw my potential, and didn't give up on me."

Chloe's eyebrows shoot up in surprise. "A mentor changed all that?"

"Yes," Shane nods, his eyes twinkling with a fond memory. "She taught me that a classroom is not just a place for instruction, but a space for growth, for connection. She showed me that being a teacher isn't about maintaining control, but about guiding young minds to discover their own paths. She was. . . Extraordinary."

Chloe is captivated, hanging onto his every word. She admires Shane's teaching style and hearing about his journey is inspiring. "She sounds incredible," she says, her voice filled with awe.

Shane smiles, his gaze softening. "She was. She was warm, kind, and inspiring. Her name was June Yearwood."

Chloe freezes, her eyes wide as she looks at Shane. "Yearwood?" she asks, her voice barely a whisper. "June Yearwood was my mother."

A soft smile spreads across Shane's face as he nods. "Yes, she was. Your mother was the one who transformed me into the teacher I am today. She helped me become Extraordinary."

Chloe is silent, her mind spinning. She was raised by her aunt and uncle and only knew that her parents died when she was 10. Over the years many of the memories faded and all she has left are pictures. She knew her mother was a respected teacher, but she had never imagined this. "I. . . I had no idea," she admits, her voice shaky.

Shane reaches out, placing a comforting hand on her shoulder. "Your mother was an Extraordinary Educator, Chloe. And she helped me become Extraordinary as well."

Shane reaches into his bag. He opens the flap to reveal *The Manual,* setting it down in front of him with a sense of reverence and respect. He places it on the table in front of Chloe and stands back as if something were about to happen.

The Manual

Chloe immediately recognizes the image embossed on the cover. "I've seen that before," she says as she simultaneously remembers. "That's the pin you guys always have on, isn't it?"

"Yep. I earned this because of everything I studied, learned, and implemented from this," Shane says as he points to the embossed name.

Chloe reads out loud, "Teach Hustle Inspire—The League of Extraordinary Educators."

She looks at Shane and then back at the manual, then back at Shane again. "What is this, some sort of secret society?" Shane looks at her with a wry smile on his face as he shrugs. "Well, sort of. The League of Extraordinary Educators was founded a long time ago," Shane explains. "Throughout history, traditional, ordinary education practices have not always been beneficial for everyone; especially people of color and those from underserved communities. Ordinary models of teaching and learning are often oppressive, and do not adequately address the diverse needs and experiences of students, whether we realize it or not. Education is supposed to be fair, equitable, and just. Unfortunately, that is not the case. The League was created to operate on principles of social justice and equity, creating a learning environment that is inclusive and welcoming to students from all backgrounds and experiences.

"Unfortunately, not everyone believes that fair education outcomes are best. There are some very powerful people who present a very real and present danger to equitable learning outcomes for our students. So the League was designed to operate within a system not designed for all students to be successful. We are trained to be everywhere and nowhere at the same time. To hide in plain sight.

"People such as me, April, and Ethan help to end ordinary by being Extraordinary educators amid the systems and policies that hold some of our best and brightest students back. We seek to give all students an education that is responsive to their needs and individual experiences, prepping them *all* for personal and academic success. All meaning just that—all."

Chloe just sits there in absolute amazement and can't believe what she is hearing. An entire secret society operating in plain sight, right under everyone's nose?

"Can I touch it?" Chloe asks hesitantly as she gestures toward the manual.

Shane pauses. "Sure, but let me show you a few things first." He opens the manual and shuffles through a few pages until he gets to a section that is handwritten and pushes it over to Chloe.

"My Ordinary Teaching?" Chloe asks inquisitively.

"Yes," Shane responds. It reads:

My Ordinary Teaching

1. Whole-class instruction is one of many methods of teaching.

2. Students should be at the center of what is taught and how. Their interests, values, and needs, not mine, are at the center of learning experiences that allow maximum engagement.

3. Worksheets should be used in moderation because they create isolated learning experiences and can limit socialization and creativity among students.

4. Disconnection is at the root of most problems.

5. Education is not inherently equitable. It is my job to recognize and value the cultural backgrounds and experiences of students and leverage this information to create a positive and inclusive learning environment.

"This one, I had to work really hard to remind myself," says Shane pointing to number four. "That's one of the things I really love about this organization, its emphasis on connection, both human-to-human and content connections. All are critical aspects of creating powerful learning experiences for students."

Shane picks up the manual, shifting the focus back to himself. "Ordinary teaching practices are designed with the curriculum in mind, and that's it. Deliver the information with the goal of transferring information, under the assumption that students will engage because they have to. Lectures, worksheets, and carrot-and-stick rewards fit right into this ordinary method of teaching with no consideration as to what reason we give for students to actually give us their attention.

"That doesn't mean the information isn't important or that the students don't want to be successful. It means that what we've come to understand as 'teaching' is more just an attempt to get students to memorize and recite facts and figures. What we fail to ask ourselves often as we teach is, what's really in it for them? What's the benefit, both immediate as well as long term, they receive? And have we made that clear to them?

"We make our students sit through lessons, day after day, where we just relay information and expect them to give us their full attention just because they're supposed to and for grades. As much as we'd like them to do that, it's simply not a good enough reason for many of them to engage. Truth be told, grades—those are for us, not them.

"And if you think about it," he goes on, "the same thing happens for us as adults. How often do we doze off in faculty meetings or fight to stay engaged during staff development? That doesn't mean that the faculty meeting or training isn't important—there is a lot of important information we need in each of these circumstances, but the information-centered approach, one that operates under the assumption that our attention should be given just because—is a tough ask."

Chloe sits back and thinks about what Shane is saying. She is really trying to process everything he said. She thinks back to plenty of times where she and Ian sat in the back of faculty meetings and giggled at inside jokes. Or how just two weeks ago she fell asleep during a professional development workshop. Although she doesn't want to admit it, she knows he is right.

"As a part of the League of Extraordinary Educators," Shane explains, "you learn about yourself first. How you interpret and respond to challenges, your behavior tendencies, how you influence others, your response to rules and procedures and patterns of behavior. You then in turn learn these details about your students and leverage this to influence their behavior and attitude.

"We understand that ordinary ways of teaching and motivating students simply do not work and we do not try to make them work. Our focus is on connection as a foundation for how we motivate students.

"Take a look at this," Shane says, pointing to a diagram in the manual. "We are trained in the art of Extraordinary Connections."

Chloe looks at the following diagram:

EXTRAORDINARY CONNECTIONS FOR TRANSFORMATIONAL TEACHING

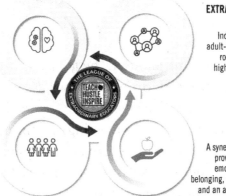

EXTRAORDINARY LEARNING EXPERIENCES
Deep, culturally significant learning experiences that authentically engage and foster equitable academic outcomes

EXTRAORDINARY TEACHER CONNECTIONS
Individualized and positive adult-to-student relationships rooted in warmth, rapport, high expectations, and trust

EXTRAORDINARY PEER COLLABORATION
Positive, mutually beneficial relationships with peers who can rely on one another to work together and contribute to the community

EXTRAORDINARY ENVIRONMENTAL CONDITIONS
A synergistic environment that provides physical as well as emotional safety, promoting belonging, motivation, enthusiasm, and an authentic love of learning

Let me ask you a question," Shane says, shifting the attention back to himself. "Do you wear glasses?"

Confused, Chloe answers, "No."

"Well, perhaps you should. I do," Shane says as he smirks and points toward his spectacles.

"But I just had my eyes checked," Chloe replies.

"No, not in that sense," Shane says. "These are not to help you see in that sense. These are for extraordinary vision."

"Extraordinary vision? What is that?" Chloe inquires.

"It's an entirely new perspective on what it means to teach," Shane explains. "As Extraordinary educators, we don't see things the same. We can't. Being Extraordinary helps us see things differently. We see our lessons differently, we see our students differently, we see ourselves differently, and we see our classrooms differently. And because we see things differently, we get different results."

Chloe takes in all of this information but is still in disbelief that this is happening.

"So," Shane pauses, "what do you think?"

Are You In?

"It's a lot to learn," Shane admits. "But it will change your life, and the life of your students. I guarantee you that."

Shane looks at Chloe and lets her process all of this for a moment. She looks at the manual, turns it over, looks back up at Shane, then back down again at the manual amazed, confused, and surprised all at the same time.

"So what do you think?" Shane proceeds "Are you in?"

Chloe pauses, thinks about it, then hands him back the manual.

"Thanks," she say. "I appreciate you telling me all of this, but this is just a lot to handle right now and I can't afford to spend the extra time it will take to learn all of this."

"Can't afford to spend the time?" Shane asks, one eyebrow raised. "So you want to continue to struggle to keep students engaged, reteach the lessons you've already taught again and again, promote mediocre levels of achievement, and hold on to that frustration of teaching in a flawed system? Sounds to me like you can't afford to keep being ordinary."

Shane closes the manual, places it back in his bag, and starts for the door. As he makes his way to open it, he stops, and he turns around to look at Chloe one more time as if to ask, "Are you sure?" Chloe does not change her position, so Shane continues out of the room.

Still in a bit of disbelief about an entire secret society right under her nose, she can't move past Shane's last words. She is actually offended at what he said. Chloe knows she is trying her hardest and for him to say that made her feel as if she isn't a good teacher. She also remembers what he said prior to that. It is a flawed system. And if you put a good person in a bad system, the system will win every time.

Unless you disrupt the system.

Typically on the ride home she uses her music or favorite podcasts to decompress from the day. This time, she drives in silence as she replays the afternoon's events over and over in her head. What else is in the manual? What is it like to be a part of the League? How would that change her as an educator or even as a person?

The next morning, Chloe walks down the hall toward her room. She tries to use the other students in the hallway as a cover but that does not work.

"Good morning, Ms. Yearwood," Shane says as he stands outside of his room with April and Ethan. She just looks at them and grins sheepishly as she tries to walk by as quickly as possible. Standing there with their League glasses and pins, which seem to stand out even more now, she knows that they know.

Chloe goes on with her day. She teaches her ordinary lessons in her ordinary way and doesn't really think much else about it. That afternoon she is giving her students some last-minute reminders as they begin to prepare for dismissal. The announcements are going to start at any moment. As she makes her way back to her desk, that pink book bag with the black stripes catches her eye. She remembers what Shane said about Mya. Chloe can't help but think about how much of a struggle it must be for Mya to be in that position. Her book bag, full of food for her family, lying there, guarded underneath her desk.

She starts to think about Mya and her habits as a student. Mya does okay, but deep down Chloe knows there is so much more to her that she just has not been able to tap into yet. What will happen if she never figures out how to unearth what she knows is inside of Mya? What will happen if Mya struggles in school and does not graduate? Would this cycle continue for her? For her family?

The students make their way down the hall, toward the buses. All Chloe can think about is how she has to do something. She can't just sit back and let Mya or any of her other students suffer anymore. If there is something that can be done, she is going to do it.

With an air of determination, she marches right to Shane's room. On the way to his car, Chloe meets him in the hallway. Before Shane can even say anything, Chloe declares, "This can't continue. I'm in."

Shane smiles and slowly nods in approval. "Good," he says and walks away.

Chloe, very confused, stands there for a moment and turns to watch Shane continue down the hallway and out the door. Did he not hear her? Is she too late? That was not the response she anticipated.

She continues with the rest of her afternoon. She gathers her materials, grabs her coat, and starts for the door. She is going to be sure to speak to Shane again tomorrow because clearly he misunderstood her.

Just as Chloe parks her car in front of her home, exhausted from another day, she hears the hum of her phone vibrating. Two short, distinct pulses indicate she has received a text message.

Puzzled, Chloe looks because she doesn't recognize the number. She taps on the icon to open the message. It reads:

> *NW corner of University Blvd & 6th Ave, 1 hour*
> *—Shane*

The Secret Society

Chloe cautiously approaches the intersection, looking around for any sign of Shane. Not seeing anything, she stops, puts the car in park, and continues to search.

Buzz-buzz. Her phone notifies her of another text message. She opens her messaging app to see another message from Shane. It reads:

> *Leave your car here and get in with us.*

Confused she thinks, "Get in with us? Who is us, and get in what?"

Just as she mutters those words, she looks up and sees a black vehicle on the other side of the street. She knows good and well that car was not there just a second ago. She sits there for a moment to try and see who is in the car. She looks a little closer and can see Shane in the driver's seat motioning for her to join him.

Closing the door as she gets out of her car, she briskly walks across the street, but as she approaches the car, her pace slows down from a brisk walk to a cautious examination of the vehicle. She can see Shane, and as she gets closer, she sees Ethan and April in the back seat. Shane rolls down the passenger side window, smiles, and says, "Hey, Chloe, come on and get in."

That eases her mind a little bit, but at this point, her heart rate is already elevated. While she knows and trusts Shane, she is prepared to jump out of that car and run for her life if she has to.

She closes the door as she sits down. Shane, putting the car in drive, pulls off and starts down the main road; no one says a word. Chloe clasps her seatbelt and sits back as they make their way. She has no idea where they are going or why she is in that car. Her uneasiness is confirmed as she begins to feel that her lunch will soon make its way to the floor as her stomach churns. Although only 2 minutes have passed, the mysterious silence of the four passengers makes it feel like an eternity for Chloe.

"I hope you don't mind, but we wanted to show you something," Shane says, finally breaking the silence.

"Sure, um, okay," Chloe replies. "Where are we going?" She is unsuccessful at hiding the tremble in her voice.

"We want to introduce you to some of our Extraordinary colleagues," April says from the back seat. "We told them all about you, and they are really interested in meeting you."

Chloe responds with a smile that veils both fear and confusion.

They approach an old four-story brick building. Making their way around the back, Shane drives up to a gate, swipes a badge, and the arm of the gate quickly rises, providing access to the lower level parking garage. A dozen or so cars are in the garage of this unassuming brick building. It has no sign, no lights, and no indication that anything has taken place there in the last 10 to 15 years.

"Okay, we're here," Shane says, turning off the ignition. Shane, Ethan, and April get out of the car, but Chloe just sits there. Shane comes around to the passenger side. He opens the door and extends his hand in a reassuring manner to let Chloe know that everything is okay and to trust him.

As she gets out of the car, she notices that all three of them have on not just the same glasses, but the same black cardigan sweater as well. They are well-fitting, neatly pressed garments with four gold stripes on the left sleeve. In the chest area on the right side of each she sees that same crest as their pin: "Teach Hustle Inspire—The League of Extraordinary Educators."

Ethan, April, and Shane all smile at Chloe and walk with her as they make their way into this mysterious building. She begins to feel a little more comfortable but is still ready to make a dash for the nearest exit if she has to.

They make their way to an elevator; Shane pushes the button for level 2. As they make their exit from the elevator, it looks totally different from what Chloe is expecting. The inside most certainly does not match the outside. This is a really nice, well-lit, vibrant facility, busy with the sounds of people.

"Hi, Chloe," the receptionist says.

Caught off guard, Chloe gives an awkward wave and "Hi" back.

"This way," Shane directs as he makes his way down a hallway. Shane opens the door to reveal a training room. Four other people with the same glasses and cardigan sweater and about a dozen other people are sitting down at narrow, conference room tables in the middle of the room.

Chloe sees her name in the second row. Shane gestures for her to join the rest of the group and take a seat as he, April, Ethan, and the rest of the Extraordinary members stand along the side.

Chloe slowly and hesitantly sits down. Then she looks at the others beside her and then at the people seated behind her as well. She looks back over at Shane, and he signals "it's okay" with a reassuring smile.

Suddenly a strong yet inviting voice calls from the front of the room, grabbing everyone's attention. "Good afternoon, fellow educators. Welcome to Extraordinary!"

Welcome to Extraordinary

"You are here not only to step into, but advance your calling. Education needs the best and the brightest to lead and teach the children of our future," the loud voice says from the front of the room. Known only as the Prime Pedagogue, the male voice speaks in a way that is commanding, yet sincere. All attention is on the front of the room as he speaks with authority and urgency.

"You will be trained in the art of Extraordinary Connections," he continues. "If you pass and meet all of the training requirements, you will join us among the ranks of an elite, stealth, and world-changing organization: The League of Extraordinary Educators."

One by one, the League members begin handing out small cases to the new recruits. The members place the cases in front of each recruit and return to their places along the edge of the room.

"As new recruits, one of the first things you must do is change your perspective. You cannot continue to see things the same way you did before. Each one of you has been given League spectacles because as a part of the League we cannot see things the same. We see our lessons differently, we see our students differently, we see ourselves differently, and we see our classrooms differently. And because we see things differently, we get different results."

Each of the new recruits reaches forward to reveal their new glasses. Chloe examines hers as she removes them from the box. She looks back over at Shane, and he smiles. She can't help but to broach a smile; although this is a new and unique experience, she instantly feels a renewed sense of calling as an educator. Slowly, each of the new recruits puts on the glasses, looking around at one another.

The Prime Pedagogue continues, "Educators have the most important profession on the face of this planet. There exists no other that has this level of influence on so many lives. You are here because we believe in you. But you must prove that you believe in you and that we can count on you in this critical fight. You will be required to pass a series of academic and well as psychological evaluations to demonstrate the competence and skills needed to be Extraordinary.

"If you pass your training, you will join us as a part of an elite organization charged with changing the world. We face the difficult task of teaching the best and brightest students of the future, amid a very real and present danger in our schools: the Education Preservation Alliance."

The recruits almost all simultaneously display looks of concern and worry as he continues.

"From the outside, the Education Preservation Alliance appears as a group of good Samaritans," the Prime Pedagogue begins, his voice steady and calm. "They wear the guise of concerned citizens fighting for children. They speak of tradition and standards, and they paint themselves as protectors of education.

"But what they don't tell you is that their preservation is selective. It works only for the chosen few, for those born into the 'right' ZIP codes, into the 'right' families. It's an alliance rooted in advantage and power, an alliance that thrives on maintaining the status quo."

He takes a moment to let his words sink in, his gaze meeting each recruit's eyes. The Education Preservation Alliance is a powerful group, and he wants each recruit to understand this. The organization has a vested interest in maintaining the status quo for educational policies and laws—policies, rules, and laws that inherently oppress some of the best and brightest in classrooms across the country. Their influence on federal, state, and local laws and policies has left generations upon generations of children excluded from academic success because it disproportionately benefits children who come from advantaged backgrounds.

"The Education Preservation Alliance," the Prime Pedagogue continues, "works to generate fear, disseminating disinformation about innovative teaching methods and pedagogies, particularly those that advocate diversity and inclusivity, labeling them as 'experimental' and 'risky.' They are skilled at shifting the blame for educational disparities onto families, communities, and even teachers, steering the public's attention away from systemic inequities that they help maintain.

"What we have learned is the key to their strategy has been disconnection. As long as they continue to seed policies and standards that fuel a system of disconnect for our students, we will continue to see low levels of achievement and frustrated teachers, leaving success only available to the advantaged.

The Prime Pedagogue pauses for a moment, taking a very intentional moment to look each and every recruit in the eye. "They are counting on you to be ordinary," he says with every bit of sincerity and urgency in his voice. "We train you to be transformative amid a system that was not designed for all children to be successful. Because the Education Preservation Alliance is so powerful, we must exist among the shadows."

Now he steps closer to the recruits. "We are defenders of equity. We are disruptors of ordinary. We are everywhere and nowhere at the same time. We are the League of Extraordinary Educators."

With that statement, some of the current League members begin to move toward the recruits. Shane makes his way over to Chloe, holding a book.

"Your Connection Mentor will now give you your manual. Let it guide you, let it empower you. Guard it with your life."

The new recruits all carefully and cautiously examine their newfound tool. Just like the one Shane had, Chloe looks at the one she now holds and knows she will do everything she can to protect it. Chloe opens up her manual to find "The Core Tenets of the League of Extraordinary Educators." It reads:

The Core Tenets of the League of Extraordinary Educators

As members of the League of Extraordinary Educators, we have a responsibility to lead the way toward fair, high-quality education for all students. We value student funds of knowledge, the often overlooked assets right in our classrooms. We seek, find, and use what works to advance student achievement with the goal of creating equitable learning opportunities for all students.

Instead of ordinary standards and objectives, Extraordinary educators see an opportunity for Extraordinary Learning Experiences: Deep, culturally significant learning experiences that authentically engage and foster equitable academic outcomes.

Instead of disconnected, individualized experiences, Extraordinary educators see an opportunity for Extraordinary Peer Collaboration: Positive, mutually beneficial relationships with peers who can rely on one another to work together and contribute to the community.

Instead of lowering expectations and focusing solely on the content to be taught, Extraordinary educators see an opportunity for Extraordinary Teacher Connections: Individualized and positive adult-to-student relationships rooted in warmth, rapport, high expectations, and trust.

Instead of an atmosphere of disconnection, oppression, and an air of survival, Extraordinary educators see an opportunity for Extraordinary Environmental Conditions: A synergistic environment that provides physical as well as emotional safety, promoting belonging, motivation, enthusiasm, and an authentic love of learning.

The Prime Pedagogue continues, "It is important you all learn and embody the League's Creed. This is our North Star. It guides what we do and why we do it. Please turn to page 4 in your manual, stand, and recite it with me."

One by one the new recruits stand to join the other League members on their feet. As the new recruits read, the League members proudly recite the following creed:

The League Creed

I am on a mission for fair and equitable education.
I am on a mission for love, connection, and a first-class learning experience.
I am on a mission to deliver education for life, and education for all.
All meaning ALL!

There is an air of nervousness, but excitement in the room. The League members and new recruits are charged and ready to change the world. Shane looks at Chloe and smiles. She glances at him, returns the smile, then looks around at her follow recruits, all of whom are smiling too.

Returning the focus to the front, the Prime Pedagogue ushers the new recruits to take their seats. "We see very good things in your future, as well as for your students. But this is just the beginning. As teachers, you have a profession. As Extraordinary educators, you step into your calling. Welcome to Extraordinary."

Preparing for Extraordinary

In the coming days, Chloe engages in a series of rigorous and challenging tests and evaluations. The League begins with a series of psychological assessments to measure the new recruits' abilities to maintain their composure in high-pressure situations. Chloe, who is not the best at handling stress, goes through several simulations where she is challenged to anticipate and manage her stress levels among some very challenging scenarios. But this allows her to truly understand how she responds in certain situations because she is given the tools to handle these issues.

Chloe is also assessed on her emotional intelligence to measure her ability to recognize, understand, and manage her own emotions, as well as the emotions of others. This consists of a series of self-reported questionnaires she is to respond to. Giving her a baseline for her self-awareness, self-management, social awareness, and relationship management, she has several performance-based tasks to help build her skills in this area. These tasks include interpreting tonality, reading body language, and correctly identifying the emotions of others from varying cultures and backgrounds. This is especially challenging for Chloe, as she never really considered these things in others and how it plays into her interactions with them.

Chloe is given consistent feedback on her emotional intelligence. She shows strengths in some areas and limitations in others. However, the League trainers encourage her and let her know that, with intent and consistency, she'll have Extraordinary emotional intelligence in no time. Chloe is very intentional as she puts her new skills into practice. With the various simulations in the League training facility, as well as what she puts into practice in her own classroom, she is able to demonstrate significantly improved levels of emotional intelligence in managing conflicts, building trust, understanding and adapting to different cultural norms, and even repairing past relationships that had been damaged in one way or another.

In order for the League of Extraordinary Educators to maintain its level of secrecy, Chloe and the other new recruits are required to pass rigorous trainings on security and discretion. The League trainers make it very clear what is at stake. They regularly reiterate the importance of securing classified information and likely consequences of compromised documents. New recruits are given the League guidelines for classification levels and different types of information that accompany each. There is also extensive training on how to appropriately handle, store, delete, and transmit classified League documents, including how to operate secure lines of communication and end-to-end system encryption methods.

Chloe's training also dives into the realm of cognitive science, specifically focusing on the science of learning and information processing in the brain. This is a completely new territory for Chloe, who has never before considered the complex neural mechanisms that are at play while she is teaching. As her trainers explain, understanding how the human brain processes, retains, and recalls information is paramount to becoming an Extraordinary educator.

"The science of learning," the Prime Pedagogue explains, "is an interdisciplinary field that explores the processes involved in learning. It encompasses cognitive science, educational psychology, and neuroscience."

Chloe is fascinated to learn about the various learning strategies that have been validated by scientific research, such as spaced repetition, interleaving, and retrieval practice. She finds herself captivated by the notion that, by understanding the mechanisms behind these strategies, she can dramatically enhance her students' ability to retain and recall information.

The concept of information processing in the brain is unfolded to her. This theory likens the brain to a complex computer that processes, stores, and retrieves information. Chloe learns how the brain encodes sensory information, processes it in the working memory, and then transfers it to long-term memory. She is introduced to the limitations of working memory and the importance of reducing cognitive load in her classroom.

As Chloe delves into these concepts, she feels a sense of empowerment and excitement. She is intrigued by the idea that she can leverage these scientific insights to revolutionize her teaching methods.

It is a lot of information for Chloe to handle, but she is managing well. As her Connection Mentor, Shane is responsible for Chloe and her progress. He often asks her random questions about League protocols and discretion measures while at school. In one instance he walks up behind her and attempts to grab her manual out of her bag. Before he can even get near the book, she firmly grabs his hand without even looking. Chloe looks to see whose hand she is holding on to, recognizing it is Shane.

"Just making sure you're on your toes," he says as they both laugh. "How's everything going? You're doing really well with your training."

"I'm hanging in there." Chloe replies. "It's a lot, I must admit, but I am really enjoying this challenge and what I'm learning as a result."

"Great," Shane says. "Glad to hear that, because things are about to get more interesting."

The Letter

To become a part of the League of Extraordinary Educators, Chloe finds herself in the middle of a very transformative, eye-opening, and challenging, yet rewarding experience. The information she is learning would undoubtedly help her as she grows professionally and personally. She really likes that the League emphasizes this journey as a quest for fulfillment.

They spend a considerable amount of time examining what fulfillment is and more importantly what it looks like in each of their lives. To finish out this phase of the training, each new recruit is tasked with adding their personal thoughts on fulfillment to their manuals. Chloe's response is as follows:

> *I was surprised to learn that many people, including myself, have the wrong idea as to what fulfillment is. Too often, people try to supplement fulfillment with material things that are nothing more than mere temporary sources of satisfaction. All of the money, the cars, and the clothes that one could buy do not define success, nor do they create fulfillment.*
>
> *Fulfillment of life has a purpose, meaning, and a sense of satisfaction. This became so much clearer to me as I reflect back on instances of giving, community service efforts, and of course teaching. Participating in these efforts is inherently fulfilling because I am honoring my values and contributing to the lives of others in a positive way.*
>
> *This greater understanding of fulfillment is really helpful because it allows me to be more intentional about things*

Continued

Continued

> that bring me true satisfaction, like my work as an educator. It is not just a job, but my contribution to mankind. It has its challenges, like any other profession, but I find comfort in the realization that I have been functioning in a broken system this entire time. The fact that I've accomplished what I have is a miracle, and I am proud of that. I know that becoming a member of the League will help me to not only be a better educator, but a better person. Not just for my students, but for myself and my family as well.

Later, Chloe finds herself lingering after one of the training sessions, her mind still grappling with this idea of fulfillment. Shane approaches her, a small, mysterious smile on his face.

"Chloe," Shane begins, "I think it's the right time to give this to you." He extends his hand. In it is a delicately folded letter, slightly worn from time but still preserved with care.

A rush of emotions surge through Chloe as she recognizes the handwriting on the envelope. It is her mother's. Her heart pounding in her chest, she carefully unfolds the letter, her eyes scanning the words her mother had left for her.

> "My dearest Chloe, if you are reading this, it means I am long gone . . ." the letter begins. Chloe takes a deep breath, steadying herself for the words that follow.
>
> From the moment you were a little girl playing with your dolls, pretending to be their teacher, I knew you

were destined for greatness. You had a spark, a natural gift for guiding and inspiring others.

It is time you know the truth. I believe, Chloe, that education should be a positive, life-changing experience for students. I believe that every child, no matter their background, culture, or socioeconomic status, deserves to learn in an environment that nurtures their potential and celebrates their uniqueness. Clark does not share these values.

Your brother Clark, he was our first-born, our initial journey into parenthood. We were so young, barely adults ourselves, when we welcomed him into the world. We did everything we could, poured every ounce of our love and care into raising him. Our intentions were always pure, always focused on giving you all the best possible we could. I blame myself because I did the best I could as a mother but Clark still struggled. And for that, he resented me. He resented us. Clark was a complex soul. He felt things deeply, and his emotions often guided his actions, for better or worse, leading him to become a part of the Education Preservation Alliance.

When your father discovered Clark's affiliation with the Alliance, it shattered his heart. He viewed it as a personal failure, an indictment of his parenting. He felt as if he had let Clark down, as if he hadn't done enough to guide him along the right path. That guilt, that feeling of inadequacy, was a weight too heavy for him to carry. It consumed him, my love, and ultimately led to his demise.

Continued

Continued

> If you're reading this, you have a unique opportunity to not only continue the legacy of being Extraordinary, but making a difference in the lives of so many. Education can and will be better—and that is because of people just like you.
>
> All my love, Mom.

Tears well up in Chloe's eyes as she finishes reading the letter, her heart heavy yet strangely comforted by her mother's words. She looks up at Shane with an air of appreciation in her gaze. Shane smiles as he nods, "You're welcome."

Helplessness

The next week, Chloe finishes up a conversation with a fellow recruit and makes her way to her seat in the League Training facility. She is surprised to see that Shane is leading that day's session.

"Good afternoon, everyone," Shane calls. "As we begin I'd like to ask for your help. If you could please open your manual and turn to page 37 and have something to write with. You'll see the page is relatively blank, but that was done intentionally. On it you will find three spaces, and I simply want you to write three things when I ask you to."

He begins to walk around the room and hand out index cards to the class of League recruits.

"As you receive your card, please just leave it face down until I give further instructions," he says as he places one card in front of each person. Making his way back to the front, he explains what each person is to do.

"When I ask you to, turn the card over. On it you will find three anagrams. You are to solve them one at a time. Please do not move on to the next item until I ask."

"What's an anagram?" one of the recruits inquires from the left side of the room.

Shane replies, "Think of it as a word puzzle. Take the letters in one word and rearrange them to make another word. Make sense?"

The recruit nods his head.

"Good," Shane says. "Please turn your card over and solve anagram number one. When you have written down your answer in your manual please raise your hand."

The recruits turn over the index cards. Within the first 10 seconds, the recruits on the right side of the room raise their hands. As Shane makes his way around the room in observation, the recruits on the left side have confused and puzzled looks on their faces.

"Please keep your hand up once you've found the answer until we're ready to move on," Shane announces.

The recruits wait with their hands up, patiently waiting for the next challenge.

"I tell you what, let's just move on. Don't worry about the first one," Shane tells the group. "Go ahead and move to anagram number two, and just like before when you're done, please raise your hand."

Shane continues to make his way around the room. Within the first 10 seconds, the recruits on the right side of the room raise their hands, signaling they've solved the problem, just as before. And just as before, the recruits on the left side of the room look around to see their counterparts come to an answer they have yet to find.

After a moment, Shane continues, "Let's not worry about this either. Let's just move on to complete the last problem. Just as before, when you have solved the challenge please raise your hand."

And in almost a predictable fashion, the recruits on the right side of the room raise their hands once again, leaving the recruits on the left side puzzled.

Shane makes his way back to the front of the room. The frustration on the left side of the room is palpable because almost none of them were able to solve any of the puzzles. The right side, having solved all three of the items, is primed and ready for whatever is to come next.

"I have a confession," Shane announces. "You were given two different lists."

Confused, everyone looks around trying to figure out exactly the reason for the dupe.

"Each of you were given three anagrams to solve, but everyone on the right side of the room was given simple, easy-to-solve puzzles, while everyone on the left was given something different."

Shane then holds up a large poster with an example of what the left side had versus the right side. The displayed lists are as follows:

RIGHT SIDE	LEFT SIDE
1 shah	1 aordiz
2 dusty	2 rrefmoa
3 toe trios	3 toe trios

"What I did, in less than a matter of minutes, was create learned helplessness among almost everyone on the left side of the room."

Pointing to the first, simple example from the list given to the right side, Shane asks the group, "What is the correct answer for this one?"

"Hash," the group says collectively. Shane nods.

"How about this one?" He points to the second item on the right side's list.

"Study," they all say collectively.

"Here's the thing," Shane says. "While the right side had a list with two easy anagrams to start, the left side had a list with two impossible anagrams to start. But," he paused. "Both sides had the same third item."

"What's the answer to the third one?"

"Tortoise," they reply.

Feeling like his point is starting to become clear, he asks recruits from the left side, "What happened when you saw others on the right side quickly solve the problems while you struggled? How did you feel?"

Shane acknowledges one recruit who raises her hand: "I was really confused," she admits.

Another chimes in, "Yeah, as I was struggling to solve the problem, but so many others figured it out I was starting to feel rushed and frustrated, especially as we got to the second anagram."

"I bet," Shane confirms. "Now, did you notice how when we got to the third anagram, although both sides had the same puzzle, only those on the right side came up with the answer. Why was that?" he asks, directing the question at Chloe this time.

Having been one of the recruits on the left side, she says, "By the time I got to the third puzzle, I was in no way confident I'd be able to do it. I figured why try?"

"And that," Shane replies, "is what I need you all to understand. We teach in a system that was not designed for all students to be successful. When our students constantly go through learning experiences in which they are not successful, repeatedly subjected to unsuccessful learning experiences, we inadvertently put them into situations where they have the same response Chloe did. Why try?"

The new recruits are taking it all in.

Shane continues, "When we hear comments such as 'I'm not a math person' or 'I was never good at writing,' we have to understand that these are children who are communicating in no uncertain terms that nothing I do will have an effect on my performance anyway, so why try. Over a long enough period of time, what we start to see are increased levels of frustration, procrastination, and frustration, along with decreased levels of motivation, effort, and asking for help when needed."

Chloe couldn't help but to think of many instances when she saw these behaviors in her students. She even thought of her own experiences as a student where she avoided certain types of math at all costs. This was a very eye-opening experience for her and the rest of the new recruits.

Keep Up the Pace

Over the coming days, Chloe struggles with the fact that she let so many things get past her. How could she not see that so many of her students had adopted this mentality of learned helplessness? Why didn't she notice what was happening right in front of her eyes?

Shane reassures her that she didn't need to blame herself. He shares that he too had not noticed these same issues in his classroom and that she was not alone. The more she thinks about it, Chloe realizes that too often she moved too fast. She was always trying to keep up with pacing guides, with a sense of urgency she had around preparing for state assessments, not to mention her community obligations as well as her family.

Shane encourages Chloe to take a look at a specific part of the manual. He mentions that they are not going to get to it during her training, but it is there if and when it is ever needed. This particular part of the manual details what it means for people to slow down and simply "be." There is some blank space for Chloe to write her thoughts based on what she has learned. Her response is as follows:

> I've gotten so used to moving fast. I have realized that in a lot of ways, I've gotten used to the no-time-to-catch-your-breath, fast-paced culture we live in. Everything is about speed. I have lost, and have made no attempt to find, my deeper self.
>
> Growing up in a city where many of the daily interactions are so fast paced, it just seems to be the norm. I do everything in a hurry: microwaveable breakfasts eaten on the go, if I even have time to eat. I drive to work and see people shave and put on makeup in their car traffic lights. We constantly move from one activity to the other, to the other, with no break. Too many days I'm so worn out we end up ordering takeout for dinner. Some instances are worse where dinner is an "every man for himself" with no effort to eat as a family unit.
>
> I believe that a lot of this adds to high levels of stress and creates further distances from my inner self, or state of "being." However, I am making a new promise to myself that I will not trade my peace of mind and comfort to keep up with the lightning speed of everything else around me. I recognize it is not always possible to slow down and sometimes there are unavoidable instances where I must move fast. But I will make it my business to move forward knowing that everything doesn't have to be about speed. I know this will keep my stress levels down and allow me more opportunities to contact my deeper self and to simply be.

In the coming days and weeks, Chloe makes much more of an effort to be aware and present. She is conscious about what she is doing and how she is doing it. She makes sure to remind herself that it is okay to keep herself a priority.

As a result of her training with the League of Extraordinary Educators, her League glasses have started to help her see things differently as an educator. She begins to see her role differently and how she has to be intentional about significant learning experiences for her students based on their individual needs. She starts looking differently at the resources available to her and begins to think about how she can create Extraordinary learning experiences for her specific students. Having a good understanding that the brain seeks to connect what it's learning to what it already knows, and that our education system is not built to do this for all students, she begins to reflect with questions such as the following:

- How is this learning experience relevant to my students?
- Does this empower and affirm each of my students or just some?
- How am I giving students time and space to be reflective and think critically?
- Does this allow my students to understand different points of view?
- Is it possible that this is reinforcing stereotypes of any kind?
- Whose perspective might be missing from this and how can it be included?

Chloe recognizes these are critical questions to regularly ask herself as she grows from ordinary to Extraordinary.

Connection to the Content

"For the Education Preservation Alliance, ordinary is the goal and disconnection is the weapon," the League trainer announces to a room full of the new recruits. "Ordinary teaching practices fuel disconnection. Students are disconnected from one another. Students are disconnected from their teacher. Students are disconnected from a supportive environment, and students are most certainly disconnected from the learning experiences.

"The first of our League tenets is Extraordinary Learning Experiences: deep, culturally significant learning experiences that authentically engage and foster equitable academic outcomes. You are all being charged with the task of coming up with your own creative and unique way to create Extraordinary Learning Experiences for your students. You will design and implement this and report back to League Headquarters, sharing with each of your colleagues."

Chloe has absolutely no idea what she is going to do, and Shane sees it all over her face.

"What's the matter?" he asks after they've wrapped up the day's session.

"I have absolutely no idea what I am going to do for this. I mean, I understand what you all are asking, but I'm just not that creative," she says with a worried tone.

"Just give it some thought," he reassures her. "You have time."

That doesn't really help Chloe because she still feels she won't be able to meet the expectation for this challenge.

Later that evening, Chloe sits down after having a nice dinner before getting into bed. She grabs her favorite throw from the back of the couch, plops onto the sofa, and turns the TV on. Just in that instance it hits her.

At her next League training session, the League trainer invites each of the new recruits to share their creative strategies one by one. There are some awesome and unique ideas, as everyone takes notes, new recruits and seasoned League members alike. Finally, it is Chloe's turn.

"One of my absolute favorite movies is the 1994 blockbuster *Independence Day*," she began. "Although I've seen this movie literally dozens of times, if I have a moment to scroll through the channels on television and it comes across the guide, that's what I'm stopping on every time. I know the movie forward and backward and can tell you exactly what's going to happen. Yet, every single time I watch it, I am captivated by it all over again.

"So many of us have seen our favorite films, TV shows, and plays, or read our favorite books multiple times but nevertheless jump at an opportunity to indulge all over again. Even though you know what's coming, why is this happening? Is it the stunning visuals or the novel ways in which their favorite actor or actress wins them over? Although that may have a role, it is likely not the fundamental cause. This is because of the presence of a compelling story. The ability to enjoy and remember stories is innate to the human mind.

"Stories are powerful delivery mechanisms because of the easy and engaging way they can be used to relay information and ideas. In comparison to dry data or figures, these are more likely to be retained and comprehended. Our brains become more active when they listen to a story because we are making an effort to interpret what we're hearing and find connections to our own experiences.

"The ability of stories to evoke emotion and create empathy for the characters and situations they depict makes storytelling a powerful communication tool, and because it gets our emotions involved, it increases the likelihood that the story will be remembered.

"I began to think, 'What kind of reaction would I get using story as a delivery method in the classroom?' I wondered if new learning concepts could be introduced to students in a way that is both engaging to them and easy for them to remember. This turned out to be a huge success!" she says as she smiles.

"Additionally," Chloe continues, "I discovered that students who are given the opportunity to share their *own* stories develop their storytelling skills and their ability to articulate their ideas clearly and convincingly in writing. Students shared personal stories through writing, dictation, and some a combination of the two.

"I took it even further and leveraged this as a way for my students to work on their critical thinking skills too. I gave them a thought-provoking prompt based on the learning objective followed by some questions. They got to present their own interpretation of the story's events, drawing their own conclusions. It seemed to really connect with them on a deeper, emotional level and this was a learning experience they truly enjoyed. So did I."

The group applauds Chloe for an awesome presentation as she makes her way back to her seat. Shane, standing on the side smiling ear-to-ear, gives her the thumbs up and mouths, "I told you that you could do it!"

A Supportive Environment

To support Chloe in her learning to become a part of the League of Extraordinary Educators, Shane often spends time in Chloe's classroom as her mentor to help and offer suggestions when needed. Chloe really appreciates how Shane is able to offer her timely, relevant, and effective feedback to help her move further faster.

"That was a great lesson," Shane says as Chloe finishes her science hour. "Can I ask you something?" he follows up.

"Sure," Chloe says hesitantly.

"I noticed your system for recognizing students. Have you noticed that you often recognize the same students over and over?" Shane says.

Thinking for a moment, Chloe responds, "Well, sort of, yeah. It's typically the same group of students who consistently achieve at the highest levels. The others are doing the best they can and have certainly come a long way though."

"Yes, they most certainly have. It's a testament to how much your instruction has improved." Shane says. "But what can you do to reward those students too?"

Chloe thinks again. "I guess I'm not sure. What do you suggest? You're my mentor, so you have all the answers, right?" She says jokingly.

Shane laughs, "Yes, I am your mentor, but I do not have all the answers. But," he pauses on his way out of the door, "you do have a resource in your possession that does," he says upon his exit, leaving Chloe an opportunity to think and solve her own problem.

Knowing exactly what he meant, Chloe grabs her manual. Thumbing through the table of contents, she finds a section entitled "Extraordinary Environmental Conditions."

It reads as follows:

Students' motivation to succeed in school stems, in part, from their desire to satisfy their innate drive to feel like they are growing, learning, and overcoming obstacles. It is vital that the learner sees this development and triumph over adversity as meaningful. This tactic works because it meets the need for doing something useful while simultaneously creating enthusiasm because of the feeling of progress.

Instead of an atmosphere of disconnection, oppression, and an air of survival, Extraordinary educators see an opportunity for Extraordinary Environmental Conditions: A synergistic environment that provides physical as well as emotional safety, promoting belonging, motivation, enthusiasm, and an authentic love of learning.

Chloe immediately knows this is what Shane is referring to. She continues to read:

In many classrooms, students are rewarded for completing tasks such as assignments and homework by receiving classroom currency or a point system displayed on a bulletin board. In this approach, students are rewarded for reaching benchmarks in their learning and are regularly recognized for their successes. This idea uses game mechanics to make learning more fun and rewarding for students.

While recognizing student achievement with points and leaderboards, it is essential to be aware of the drawbacks of praising students for their successes. It's likely this will shift focus from the act of learning to the end result of grades. It might also encourage unhealthy levels of competition and pressure among students and exclude some groups of students. An imbalance in this area of triumph may reduce one's enthusiasm to participate in an activity for its own sake, even if it looks on the surface that the purpose is genuine. There's a risk that this may foster conformity at the expense of genuine understanding due to the learner's focus on the incentive rather than the material at hand.

Continued

Continued

When we examine this practice of rewarding students solely based on actual abilities, we can see that this is in fact a practice of ordinary teaching at work. What inevitably happens is teachers find themselves repeatedly praising the same students. Too often, those that have greater access to resources or stronger academic abilities are able to coast by with little effort, while those with greater limitations give up because they feel they have no chance of succeeding. The system of extrinsic rewards such as points, grades, class cash prizes, and so on has ingrained in them a sense of hopelessness that prevents them from trying.

To address this issue, Extraordinary educators recognize students for making progress in addition to achievement. Consider a student who has shown remarkable promise in the realm of mathematics. She consistently outperforms even the top 10% of students on exams, and she finishes her coursework quickly and easily. However, you pushed her to complete work meant for the next grade level, which prompted her to go even higher. She mustered the courage to try despite her doubts, and the hard work and determination she showed paid off when she accomplished her goal and received high marks for her efforts.

On the other hand, consider a student who has struggled with math in the past but has made great strides in recent months. This student, being recognized for his development, has just as much opportunity for recognition and rewards as the student who can perform on the next grade level. This method of celebrating wins that Extraordinary educators use acknowledges the effort of both students, no matter their abilities.

Chloe thinks about how she indeed only recognizes students for achievement instead of progress. Making this adjustment is going to be huge for her. She goes right to work adjusting her rewards system and can't wait to see how these Extraordinary Environmental Conditions will impact her students' motivation.

Taking It All In

The spring sun is shining in the classroom. The classroom is a bit noisy, but not out of control, as Chloe's students are finishing up an activity. As the students make their way back to their table groups, Chloe begins to remind them about the upcoming state assessments.

"Be sure you all get a good night's rest, as I want you to make sure you're focused and ready to go tomorrow morning."

In years past, this time of year brought a lot of stress, angst, and worry for Chloe as for one reason or another she never felt her students were ready. Not this time. Not only are they ready, but she knows they are, and *they* know they are.

She continues to offer advice and last-minute test-taking tips as she makes her way around the room, handing back the students' latest practice assessments for their state exams. She pauses in front of the pink book bag with black stripes. Holding the paper upside down and slightly folded as to exercise some discretion, she places it down on the desk and looks at Mya. A smile emerges from her face as she offers Mya congratulations.

"I'm proud of you," Chloe says. "You did a phenomenal job and I have no doubt you'll knock it out of the park tomorrow." Mya smiles from ear-to-ear with excitement and pride.

Chloe isn't sure what the future will hold for Mya but feels certain that she is headed in the right direction. Mya is positioned to finish this year strong and hit the ground running next year, far exceeding any expectations she had for herself up to that point. Mya is connected to her work, Mya is connected to her classmates, and Mya is connected to herself. She is ready for that state test and so much more.

A New Chapter

The doors open to Illumination Academy and welcome anxious and excited students to the first day of school. Teachers are lined up to greet new and returning scholars. Parents, family members, and friends smile and wave good-bye as they see their children off.

"Good morning, Ms. Yearwood," Shane calls out as he walks up the hallway.

Chloe turns around as the bright light bounces off of her shiny pin. "Hey, Shane!" she says excitedly. They catch up for a few minutes before making their way to greet their new students.

Later that afternoon, Principal Williams welcomes everyone back for their first faculty meeting of the school year. She goes over how everyone did such a good job with first-day-of-school procedures and how the students are going to be prepared for another great school year.

"We have some exciting news!" exclaims Principal Williams. "I am thrilled to announce, thanks to our collective efforts that we have not only met but surpassed the achievement scores we need. Illumination Academy will remain open!"

A round of applause and cheers erupts in the room. The energy is electric. The threat of closure is a thing of the past, replaced by a newfound confidence and a sense of achievement. Principal Williams holds up her hand, signaling for quiet. "I want to take a moment to acknowledge Chloe Yearwood," she continues, her gaze landing on Chloe. "Her dedication, her innovative approaches, and her unwavering belief in our students have turned things around for us and was the deciding factor that helped us reach this seemingly insurmountable goal. Thank you, Chloe!"

The room explodes with cheers and applause. Chloe, both amazed and smiling, stands to accept her acknowledgment. She feels a rush of pride. She thinks about the struggles, the challenges, and how her own brother, Clark, had been part of those hurdles. She knows she can't change her brother's actions, but she also knows that she won't let his choices define her journey. Her success is a testament to her determination, her dedication, and her belief in her students. Clark's path is his own, separate from hers. Overcoming those barriers and proving that every child has and can realize their potential is worth it.

Chloe looks over at Shane, and like a proud big brother, he smiles as if to say, "I knew you could do it." He points at his pin, and she looks down and points at hers because they both know what it means.

It means they are teachers who beat the odds and won't leave student success to chance. It means they are teachers who are dedicated to ridding themselves of traditionally accepted practices of education. And it means their students are going to be positioned for academic and personal success.

After the faculty meeting, Shane and Chloe make their way out of the media center when Ian walks up to Chloe. "Congratulations! Wow, you must have worked some magic in your classroom last year. We'll see if I'm lucky and get a good group like you."

Chloe looks at Shane, then back at Ian. "It's not luck at all."

"Well then, maybe you can work some of your magic on some of my students," Ian says jokingly as he laughs.

"I'd be happy to!" Chloe replies.

"Really?" he says with a smile.

"Of course!" Chloe says as she extends her hand. As Ian takes Chloe's hand to seal the deal, she says, "Hi! My name is Chloe, and I'm your Connection Mentor."

II

The Formula
for Extraordinary

Without a shadow of a doubt, I stand firm in my conviction that teachers should enjoy the extraordinary gift of teaching and students should relish the extraordinary gift of learning. And I have a feeling you do too. Teaching isn't just a job. It's a calling. It's an opportunity to shape young minds and prepare them for a future we can only imagine.

Unfortunately, what we have is a system that has not been kind to educators and has been even worse to students. The repercussions? The list is long, but let's begin with teachers who are underprepared and pushed into circumstances where exhaustion is almost a given. The pressure is overwhelming, leading to feelings of incompetence and eventually driving many to abandon the profession.

The impact on the student educational journey is possibly worse. Consider this: a journey that shapes a young life, their potential future, and the fate of our society, compromised by an education system that has failed each one of us over and over again.

So many students of color see education as a burdensome duty rather than an open door to opportunity. They see school as a place where they do not belong, a place where they are disconnected from their peers, their teachers, and the joy of learning, leaving them feeling unsupported and misunderstood. For children from diverse backgrounds, a negative school experience hinders their natural curiosity and thirst for knowledge. It breeds a culture of fear and disinterest, contributing to higher dropout rates and perpetuating a narrative about people who were never given a fair shot from the start.

And we wonder why we have so many behavior problems in our classrooms. It's human nature to resist when we feel we are not welcomed. It's human nature to avoid what we're not good at. It's no surprise, then, that students who struggle academically may engage in distracting behaviors out of frustration or boredom. This, in turn, leads to them being labeled as "problems," being put on IEPs, even suspended and expelled. This isn't addressing the issue; it's merely a manifestation of it.

Part II breaks down each element of the Extraordinary Connections. Drawing upon years of research and firsthand experience, this formula isn't pulled from thin air. It's grounded in rich fields of study, like culturally responsive pedagogy, human behavior, cognitive science, educational psychology, and neuroscience.

I'm not just looking at teaching strategies and pedagogical theories. I'm looking at how to bring joy back into the classroom, how to make learning not just an obligation, but an adventure, and how to transform a classroom from a space of ordinary into the realm of extraordinary, and not just for the students, but for teachers too.

CHAPTER
1

How We Got Here

More than a hundred years ago the entire educational system in this country was designed around the belief that children's achievement could be placed on a bell curve, and so the approach was to teach to the middle. Teach the average child.

The U.S. Department of Education created policies, laws, and federal guidelines around education based on that principle. The individual states' education agencies then determined criteria for teacher certification based on federal education guidelines. College and university teacher preparation programs created pathways for aspiring educators to get certified based on state mandates as well as district hiring qualifications as a direct result of state laws.

What we have are teacher training and preparation programs built on state standards that are the result of federal mandates. The federal education guidelines made way for a standardized, one-size-fits-all method of teaching children. The focus was on memorization of facts as opposed to mastery, and regurgitating content instead of creative problem-solving. Federal guidelines focused on the "average" child, not any science or research on human behavior, learning, or development.

The result? Well, if a third of United States public school students performed well enough to get into college, it was considered a success.

Not most students. Not even half. A third.

This inevitably leaves us with three things—preparing teachers in ordinary ways, to teach ordinary lessons, and getting ordinary results. We end up with a nation of fully certified, ready and willing educators in classrooms across the country prepared for the ordinary.

Normally the term *ordinary* can be okay. Acceptable, good enough. Unfortunately, when it comes to education in the United States, ordinary is far from good enough. Ordinary is at the root of many of the complex issues and problems in our classrooms. These habits, practices, structures, thought processes, and methods have been the cornerstone of education in the United States for more than a century. You know that all too familiar setup where the teacher stands in front of the class, delivering a lecture on the topic of the hour. And, of course, all students are expected to listen attentively, demonstrate intense focus at all times, and learn at the highest levels with these methods. Works just like it's supposed to, right?

One of the biggest characteristics of these ordinary practices is that they often facilitate an environment that is very rigid and oppressive, whether you realize it or not. These ordinary practices are ineffective, severely inequitable, and directly correlate to a lack of student engagement and motivation and, therefore, low levels of achievement. They do not address the diverse needs and experiences of students. They do not take advantage of what we've come to understand about how the brain processes information. And as a result of this, connections at all levels are treated as an "if there's time" component.

Many classrooms that employ ordinary practices find that students depend on the teacher for knowledge, give no effort for challenging tasks, and demonstrate low levels of academic achievement. This leads right into the twenty-first century, where traditionally accepted practices of education have left us with students ill-prepared for real-world situations where they will need to think critically and solve problems independently.

Fundamentally, ordinary practices fuel disconnection. Students are disconnected from their learning experiences. Students are disconnected from one another. Students are disconnected from their teachers, and students are most definitely disconnected from a supportive environment.

The history of our education system has left generations upon generations of children excluded from academic success because it disproportionately benefited children who came from advantaged backgrounds. Children who fell outside of this restrictive average were essentially set up to be excluded from a fair education and learning experiences, which severely limits their chances for a successful higher education experience or adult success. This design weeded out those who did not make the cut, instead of positioning all students to be successful.

> *Fundamentally, ordinary practices fuel disconnection. Students are disconnected from their learning experiences. Students are disconnected from one another. Students are disconnected from their teachers, and students are most definitely disconnected from a supportive environment.*

Teachers can only do what they've been trained to do. Having worked with thousands of educators in different cities and schools across this country, I quite often see educators who are on the brink of defeat. They became educators because they truly enjoy the craft, love working with young people, and truly have a heart to serve. Yet, I constantly see teachers across the country who are trying to find a spark to keep going.

As an educator, what you have to realize is that "ordinary" puts us in a position that is inherently more complicated, stressful, confusing, and downright uninspiring. It always leaves us in a position where we carry the burden of instruction.

The Burden of Instruction

A huge, although familiar, part of why ordinary practices are ineffective is because of what I call the *burden of instruction*. What I've found is that in most classrooms, the teacher does the heavy lifting. The heavy lifting of being the primary source of information. The heavy lifting of having to push students to engage. The heavy lifting of trying to get students to make any sort of effort. The heavy lifting of teaching, reteaching, and in some instances reteaching concepts and standards that students need to learn.

With this burden, most, if not all, of the responsibility and effort fall on the teacher. It is a constant imbalance of effort and uphill battles from the teacher to try and persuade, push, influence, and inspire students to engage and achieve academically. This takes place day after day, week after week, month after month, and year after year. Beyond being exhausting, it is highly inefficient and directly contributes to teacher burnout and lack of job satisfaction.

One of the most common ways teachers attempt to alleviate the burden of instruction is through motivation. We all know we need and appreciate motivation, and this goes for students too. So often, when we have students who are disengaged and not performing up to their potential, we employ a number of motivation tactics.

We offer rewards or incentives to motivate students to engage, behave, and achieve specific academic goals: stickers, candy, certificates, prizes, pizza parties—you name it. I for one kept quite the stash of Starbursts in my desk and used them more often than I'm willing to admit as a source of motivation.

Sometimes point systems are used to influence student effort and academic achievement, a system where students are given points for specific behavior or actions, such as turning in an assignment on time or standing quietly in line. And how can we forget one of the most commonly used methods to influence student academic behavior—grades.

Why Manipulation Does Not Work

Here's where we're going wrong. With certain types of motivation, even if your intentions are in the right place, you can find your efforts falling flat. That heavy lifting gets heavier. It's often not too long before that candy doesn't have the same power it once did or that sticker just isn't as appealing as it once was. Moreover, what happens when the candy, stickers, and pizza parties are altogether not an option?

What we must understand and accept is that most of what we've come to know as motivation is actually manipulation. Manipulation is all about influencing the behavior of someone else to serve a purpose that (often) benefits you. Manipulation is not necessarily a bad thing because there can also be a benefit for the other person as well. For example, we want children to eat all of their vegetables at dinner so we dangle the opportunity to enjoy a sweet treat once that obligation has been met. Although it benefits you (a successful parenting act) and the child (healthy food), it is technically manipulation. These practices exist in many ways all around us, so it's not hard to see why it's so common.

What we must understand and accept is that most of what we've come to know as motivation is actually manipulation.

You've had your eye on a nice shirt for quite some time, and it's on sale so now you buy it. Manipulation. A countdown timer on the checkout page of an online shopping platform encouraging you to make that purchase before the clock hits 00:00. Manipulation. The radio host giving away front row seats to your favorite performer's next concert, but only to the 10th caller. Manipulation.

Manipulation gets results, let's be honest. But the issue is that while it gets results, it doesn't work because it isn't reliable. Here's what I mean—often manipulation is very good at gaining short-term success, but it does not achieve the long-term dedication and effort that are needed for academic success. Manipulation can be effective at positioning students to raise their hand before asking a question, but not so effective at positioning students to demonstrate high levels of creativity or use their imagination to solve problems. Manipulation might be effective at helping students to stand in a line and walk down the hallway quietly, but it will not build students' capacity to demonstrate courage and resolve when faced with academic or even personal challenges.

While manipulation is commonly used in the learning environment, we've made the assumption that because it is effective for short-term gains, it can be just as impactful for long-term gains. Instead of fostering a deep understanding and passion for learning, manipulation turns education into a transactional process, where students act based on external factors rather than genuine interest or understanding.

Teachers find themselves in a daily fight to keep students engaged during instruction. Students end up disengaged, which puts educators in a position where they constantly have to reteach the lessons they already taught several times. This perpetuates low levels of academic achievement, widening achievement gaps. This inevitably turns into teachers living in the frustration of not seeing the fruits of their labor because they work so hard, yet it rarely ever seems to pay off. Operating in a flawed system, teachers end up burned out, with no answers, constantly putting a strain on their professional and personal lives.

Our efforts to influence student academic behavior must align with what *truly* moves students forward. We do that by positioning students to see the value of learning—what's in it for them—and thereby reducing the burden.

Alleviating the Burden

To effectively reduce the burden, the first thing we have to do is understand the burden. A lot of the instructional burden comes from the effort it takes to persuade or influence students to put forth the effort necessary to attempt challenging tasks. Often, our focus is on the action, reaction, or sometimes inaction of students. However, it is vital to understand the series of events that takes place to lead to those outcomes.

What do I mean by this? Well, think of it like this. For each and every student learning opportunity, their results are the outcome of their actions. Their actions are the outcome of their emotions. Their emotions are the outcomes of their perception. Their perceptions are triggered by the conditions.

What does that mean? Let's break it down.

Conditions

Technically speaking, the conditions of a learning experience are an objective and neutral occurrence. Conditions or circumstances can often be measured, objectively proven, and fact-based. Conditions themselves are not inherently "good" or "bad." It is the student's perception of the conditions that determine this. For example, the fact that students are independently reading for 15 minutes is a condition. It can be measured, objectively proven, and fact-based. Make sense so far? Good.

Perception

Perception, however, is all about what the student *thinks* as a result of the condition. An example of this is thinking, "I don't like this." This is the personal opinion of a student, which others may or may not necessarily share. This perception is not a condition because it includes subjective judgment. Even if the entire rest of the class shares this same thought, "I don't like this," it remains a perception because it is not an objective truth. Any time a personal interpretation of a situation exists, it can be classified as a perception. Still with me?

Emotions

Now, what results from perceptions? Emotions. What students think about something determines how they feel. For example, in class, a student is asked how she feels about the chapter book the class is reading. The student responds, "I feel overwhelmed." The fact that it is a chapter book is not inherently too overwhelming; it is a neutral circumstance. However, it is the student's interpretation that the book is too long or too hard to understand that is causing the emotion of feeling overwhelmed.

It is important not to mix up or combine perception and feelings because that is a crucial factor in what moves students to do or not do certain things. Perception is what students see from their vantage point, and emotion is how they feel as a result of what they see.

Actions

Amid the classroom conditions, students will filter these circumstances through their own perceptions, and the perception causes specific emotions. As much as we want to believe we are inherently logical beings who occasionally get caught up in our emotions, it is actually the opposite. We are highly emotional beings who act based on how we feel.

In this same classroom, if the student is feeling overwhelmed after being given a chapter book to read, the student may procrastinate in order to avoid reading the book. Or the student may choose another activity, which can distract the student's peers. That emotion of feeling overwhelmed drives the action of avoidance. All student actions, inactions, and reactions are driven by the emotions that precede them. This is critical to understand. What does this lead to? You guessed it.

Results

Results are the outcomes of student action, inaction, or reaction. Because the student perceived the chapter book as overwhelming, she chose to avoid that task altogether. This can result in not meeting class participation expectations, not comprehending the content, being ill-prepared for upcoming assessments, lower academic performance, and so on.

What is essential to understand is that this pattern of conditions, perception, emotions, actions, and results is always in play.

Always. In the learning environment, any result that you observe is without a doubt preceded by an action, which was derived from an emotion, which came from the student's perception, which was triggered by the conditions.

A common practice in our profession is, when we see students struggle (for example, not demonstrating the highest levels of engagement or achievement), our intervention efforts go straight to what's observable—actions and results.

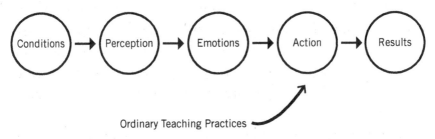

We offer support that includes reteaching or trying to explain the subject matter in a different way or a host of other intervention efforts. In each of these instances, we still end up bearing the burden of instruction. Moreover, we rarely get the results we are looking for because we find it difficult to tap into our students' full capabilities.

I know that teachers want what's best for their students and genuinely put their best foot forward to help their students achieve success. But too often, they end up with results that do not match the input. The constant disconnect that ordinary practices fuel always leaves us bearing this huge burden of instruction. The question then becomes, how? How do we help all our students be successful? How do we figure out and take advantage of what works to end ordinary practices? The answer lies in what I call Extraordinary Connections.

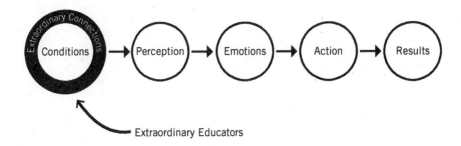

Extraordinary Educators

Extraordinary Educator Invitation to Reflect

Take this moment to think about the current state of education and how we got here:

- What are the consequences of solely relying on manipulation as a form of influencing student behavior? How can you minimize the use of manipulation in the classroom?

- How has the sequence of "conditions, perception, emotions, actions, and results" shown up in your classroom?

- How does the current educational system contribute to inequity? Where have you seen examples of this?

- How does this challenge or confirm your own views on effective teaching and learning practices?

CHAPTER

2

Becoming Extraordinary

Can I be honest for a moment? In the fable section, "An Ordinary Educator," Shane's story was my story. Shane talks about how he started his first year of teaching 6 weeks into the school year and how he already decided what type of students he was dealing with even before he met them. That was me. For 2 years I was the educator who walked into the classroom internalizing every narrative and negative thing I heard about my students and the neighborhood they lived in. For 2 years I was very cold, disconnected, and often overly assertive with my students. For 2 years I yelled a lot because I was the educator who prioritized discipline over relationships. For 2 years that's what I thought "good teaching" was. And it cost me.

Now, fast forward to my fourth year of teaching. I was being recognized by my school district for my students' exceptionally high level of achievement. I received this honor because the year prior my students did so well, they received state-level recognition. In just my fourth year of teaching, I had helped my students outperform the narratives that loomed over that building. I helped them outperform the pervasive stereotypes of the neighborhood that had long cast a shadow of doubt and limitations. The neighborhood, often misunderstood and underestimated, had been written off as a place where dreams were stifled and futures were compromised. But my students turned those shadows into stepping stones, those doubts into determination, and those limitations into launchpads.

In just my fourth year of teaching, my students proved that the power to define their futures resides not in the narratives of their surroundings, but in the determination of their spirits, in the tenacity of their will, and in the brilliance of their minds. They proved that the narratives surrounding us are not as powerful as the narratives within us.

When I began to really think about it, what this experience taught me was something very simple. They can do it. With the right approach, I was able to help my students do what was not common in that school or city. It taught me that they were just as capable as the students in surrounding, more advantaged areas. However, if I wanted better outcomes, I myself had to be better. Using ordinary approaches was not the way to get the job done. I had to rise above the circumstances. I had to rise above what was done in the past. I had to rise above ordinary.

After receiving that award, I began to see what was possible for these students whose lives I was touching on a daily basis. I began to see what was possible for me as far as my personal and professional growth. And it was extremely exciting because I knew that I was making a difference in the lives of these children, which was making a difference in the community, which was making a difference in the world.

But that showed me there was still a huge issue at hand. It was a whole 2 years that I taught with ordinary methods, and it took me entirely too long to figure out that I was operating within a system that did not inherently offer all of my students an opportunity to be successful. But how many other educators were still suffering under the gripping spell of ordinary? How many other classrooms were riddled with the gloom of disconnection that was likely well seated into the fabric of the day-to-day school experience? What is it that can be done to offer opportunities for equitable learning outcomes?

Promoting Extraordinary Connections

In its simplest terms, what I eventually learned was that if ordinary practices promote disconnection, we have to offer connection. But not just any type of connection. We have to offer Extraordinary Connections. The research on human behavior, the science of learning and development, as well as neuroscience offers very clear reasons as to why ordinary methods do not work. But more importantly, it offers incredible insight as to what does. In our classrooms, the framing and context under which learning conditions exist are the most significant factors for determining learning outcomes. In other words, the learning experiences, the human relationships, and the overall environment are critical factors. Connections must exist in each of these areas to overcome the barriers created with ordinary teaching practices. And not just any type of connections.

EXTRAORDINARY CONNECTIONS FOR TRANSFORMATIONAL TEACHING

EXTRAORDINARY LEARNING EXPERIENCES

Deep, culturally significant learning experiences that authentically engage and foster equitable academic outcomes

EXTRAORDINARY TEACHER CONNECTIONS

Individualized and positive adult-to-student relationships rooted in warmth, rapport, high expectations, and trust

EXTRAORDINARY PEER COLLABORATION

Positive, mutually beneficial relationships with peers who can rely on one another to work together and contribute to the community

EXTRAORDINARY ENVIRONMENTAL CONDITIONS

A synergistic environment that provides physical as well as emotional safety, promoting belonging, motivation, enthusiasm, and an authentic love of learning

In our classrooms, the framing and context under which learning conditions exist are the most significant factors for determining learning outcomes. In other words, the learning experiences, the human relationships, and the surrounding environment are critical factors.

With Extraordinary Connections, the focus is on the needs and interests of the students, with the intent of redistributing the burden of instruction from solely the teacher, to an even distribution between the teacher and the students. The use of these Extraordinary Connections positions us to take teaching and learning from a situation where maybe 30% of students are successful to equitable outcomes that aren't predetermined by ZIP code, cultural background, or socioeconomic status. Using these Extraordinary Connections positions us to end ordinary and become Extraordinary educators.

Seeing the Extraordinary

In the story, one of the primary reasons that members of the League of Extraordinary Educators wear glasses is because

Extraordinary educators see things differently. It is a metaphor to represent the lens through which we see education, ourselves, and our students.

- Instead of ordinary standards and objective, Extraordinary educators see an opportunity for **Extraordinary Learning Experiences:** deep, culturally significant learning experiences that authentically engage and foster equitable academic outcomes.
- Instead of disconnected, individualized experiences, Extraordinary educators see an opportunity for **Extraordinary Peer Collaboration:** positive, mutually beneficial relationships with peers who can rely on one another to work together and contribute to the community.
- Instead of lowering expectations and focusing solely on the content to be taught, Extraordinary educators see an opportunity for **Extraordinary Teacher Connections:** individualized and positive adult-to-student relationships rooted in warmth, rapport, high expectations, and trust.
- Instead of an atmosphere of disconnection, oppression, and survival, Extraordinary educators see an opportunity for **Extraordinary Environmental Conditions:** a synergistic environment that provides physical as well as emotional safety, promoting belonging, motivation, enthusiasm, and an authentic love of learning.

Getting Extraordinary Results

Because Extraordinary Educators see things differently, Extraordinary educators get different results:

- Higher levels of student engagement as a result of extraordinary learning experiences promote higher value and greater significance for students. This significantly reduces off-task behavior as well as the need to reteach with such frequency.

- Fewer classroom management issues occur because the learning environment is inherently positive and valued by the students. It is also highly engaging, minimizing opportunities for misdeeds, and fosters a strong sense of community, ownership, and good decision making.

- Stronger connections with students are a result of the intentional focus on rapport, high expectations, and trust. This allows for teachers to be perceived as someone who has students' best interest in mind and has earned the right to demand high levels of engagement and effort.

- Stress levels are lower because many of the contributing factors of ordinary teaching practices that fuel the burden of instruction are no longer an issue.

- A renewed sense of purpose as an educator allows teachers to create change, disrupt inequitable outcomes, and see the fruits of their labor as a result.

Having unveiled the transformative power of Extraordinary Connections in reshaping not only my teaching practice but the classrooms and lives of so many others, it is imperative that we explore each of these connections in greater detail. We will dissect Extraordinary Learning Experiences, Extraordinary Peer Collaboration, Extraordinary Educator Connections, and Extraordinary Environmental Conditions to understand how they weave together to redefine teaching and learning. By illuminating the intricacies of these connections, I hope to offer you practical insights to break free from the ordinary and unlock the extraordinary potential that exists within every classroom, every teacher, and every student.

Extraordinary Educator Invitation to Reflect

Take this moment to think about becoming Extraordinary:

- What is the significance in shifting your perspective about what's possible in teaching?

- How might this initial idea of Extraordinary Connections change the dynamics in your classroom or school?

- How does the author's initial assumptions and behaviors toward his students reflect societal narratives about certain groups of students?

- What does it mean to "see things differently" as an Extraordinary educator? Can you think of examples from your own practice?

- How can the concept of Extraordinary Connections be applied beyond the classroom to influence school culture or education policy more broadly?

3

Extraordinary Learning Experiences

Extraordinary Learning Experiences are deep, culturally significant learning experiences that authentically engage and foster equitable academic outcomes.

EXTRAORDINARY LEARNING EXPERIENCES

Deep, culturally significant learning experiences that authentically engage and foster equitable academic outcomes

Tell me if this sounds familiar: a designated day of professional development. You're not really sure what the session will be about, but you do know you're required to go. You gather all of your materials, make sure you have something to write with, maybe a few things to snack on, and you're all set to go. You get to the session, take your seat, and the training begins. You quickly, yet disappointingly, realize something.

Whether it is not your specific content area, something you've already learned, or it simply does not pertain to the needs, desires, or challenges you face, you easily recognize it is not relevant to your current and specific needs and therefore has little to no value for you.

So what happens? You disengage. You're not rude about it or anything, but you may pick up your phone or open your laptop and log some grades and score some homework assignments, while shuffling back and forth between social media platforms. There's no effort to pay attention, because again, there's little to no value in paying attention. There's nothing that you can take out of this, so you might as well do something else so it's not a total waste of time, right?

Encouraging Extraordinary Learning Experiences

Here's the thing: this happens to our students as well. They get into ordinary classrooms, quickly and reluctantly realizing this information doesn't pertain to the needs, desires, or challenges they face and therefore holds little to no value for them. So what happens? They disengage. But with our students, disengagement shows up in many different forms, from a lack of focus to off-task and disruptive behavior. And instead of a wasted afternoon, it's a wasted week, a wasted month, or a wasted school year. And this cycle happens over and over again. So many students have to go through learning experiences they feel have no relevance or value to their life. And of course, some do well and succeed. But we have to ask ourselves—are these students succeeding *because of* or *in spite of* ordinary teaching practices?

If you've been in a classroom more than 15 minutes, you've likely heard the question most teachers hear, "Why do we need to learn this?" As a student myself, I recall countless instances of absolute boredom that felt like academic torture: lessons about people, places, and stories I had no connection with whatsoever. For me and a lot of others, there was no significance.

If we are going to get down to the nitty-gritty of what it means to be an Extraordinary educator, we must start with Extraordinary Learning Experiences. The value of each learning experience is contingent on the extent to which it may be applied to the student's personal experiences. When students can relate to what they are learning, they are more likely to be interested in the subject matter and take an active interest in their education.

Generally, students learn better and retain information better when the learning experience leverages an emotional attachment. Think about the process described earlier: conditions, perception, emotions, actions, and results. Extraordinary Learning Experiences lay the groundwork for an emotional investment from the students, which positions students to better absorb the content and apply it in meaningful ways. The idea of Extraordinary Connections by way of Extraordinary Learning Experiences changes the focus from the end result to the learning process itself.

> *The value of each learning experience is contingent on the extent to which it may be applied to the student's personal experiences. When students can relate to what they are learning, they are more likely to be interested in the subject matter and take an active interest in their education.*

Ordinary teaching practices promote a level of disconnect from learning that is almost automatic. These traditionally accepted ways of instruction often filter content through a narrow perspective that may not be representative of the students in a given classroom. Students who cannot relate to the narrative promoted by the literature, curriculum, examples, viewpoints, and subject matter may feel that their identities and cultures are not valued or reflected in the classroom. Consequently, students sometimes get disengaged from the material being taught and lose interest in participating in the activity altogether.

Unfortunately, this has put us in a position where you can practically predict the learning outcomes of students of color as well as students from traditionally underserved communities. For students of color, going to school can be a source of anxiety and isolation if the curriculum they are being taught has no relevance to their lives.

One of the easiest and most direct ways to ensure inequitable outcomes for students is to perpetuate disconnection. Disconnection from what is learned and how it is taught is a pathway to ensure continued low levels of achievement for students and high levels of frustration for teachers.

It is so important to understand that children of all ages love to learn. The brain of a child is and has always been primed for continuous learning. The science shows us that, contrary to what we thought in the past about the abilities of children, the brain is constantly in the process of being shaped based on experiences, the environment, as well as the relationships that exist in that child's life. We know that the brain is highly malleable, meaning it can grow. However, it must be under the right circumstances, with the right support.

> *Disconnection from what is learned and how it is taught is a pathway to ensure continued low levels of achievement for students and high levels of frustration for teachers.*

Extraordinary Learning Experiences for students require teachers to actively interact with and value students' varied cultural experiences. This approach to teaching recognizes that students' cultural identities and experiences impact not only their worldviews but how they learn. Additionally, this method positions educators to take advantage of the natural cognitive and neurological processes we each have to ensure the highest levels of learning. This contributes to a learning environment that encourages curiosity and stimulates the students' senses in a variety of ways, igniting passion, curiosity, all while nurturing lifelong learners.

Extraordinary Educator Invitation to Reflect

Take this moment to think about student opportunities to connect to the content through extraordinary learning experiences.

- Are students from different backgrounds achieving at different levels?
- What can happen when Extraordinary Learning Experiences are not present in the classroom?
- Do you offer opportunities for students to see themselves in what is learned and how it is taught?
- How are students and their experiences centered in your classroom?
- Do you offer learning experiences of significance for your students where ideas, identities, and perspectives are familiar and relatable?
- Have you considered from whose perspective the information is presented and if it is the best perspective for the population of students you serve?

CHAPTER
4

Extraordinary Peer Collaboration

Extraordinary Peer Collaboration involves positive, mutually beneficial relationships with peers who can rely on one another to work together and contribute to the community.

EXTRAORDINARY PEER COLLABORATION

Positive, mutually beneficial relationships with peers who can rely on one another to work together and contribute to the community

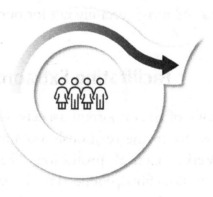

The year 2020 was an extremely difficult time for many of us. Everyone, pretty much everywhere, experienced difficult and adverse circumstances in some way, shape, or form simultaneously. We were thrust into a period where we quickly saw how the convenience of being able to see friends, family, coworkers, and the like was quickly snatched from our grasp. We had no choice but to isolate ourselves while we slowly tried to adapt to a world that was drastically changing around us.

Like many of us, we did what we could to mimic those interactions we were so used to with social media and even video conferencing events and parties. While these digital social gatherings helped pass the time and subsidized our social life, it was an obvious reminder that we need and desire relationships. Video conferencing did the job for the time being. Still, there is nothing like being in the presence of one another for a true, authentic connection. Connection is good for the soul.

Our ability to connect with others has helped our species survive. We have needed to be around and rely on one another for love, safety, and resources since the beginning of time. This is an intrinsic desire and biological need for us, and what we have to understand is that this need for connection and human-to-human interaction doesn't go away when we go to school, not for us and most certainly not for our students either.

Facilitating Extraordinary Connections

One of the important aspects of teaching is understanding that we are in the relationship-building business. Teaching is not a sterile, tactical profession. Teaching is a human-to-human, emotion-filled, connection-driven experience. We are a communal species that has survived for thousands of years due to relationships. Our brains are always seeking to connect, interact, and enjoy the presence of those around us. It is a legitimate biological need. Unfortunately, what can happen in the learning environment is that the need is not met for some students. The way the education system was designed, many students experience a similar kind of isolation in traditional classroom setups.

One of the most important aspects of teaching is understanding that we are in the relationship-building business. Teaching is not a sterile, tactical profession. Teaching is a human-to-human, emotion-filled, connection-driven experience.

One of the true superpowers of Extraordinary educators is to position students to connect with one another through Extraordinary Peer Collaboration. This is a purposeful positioning of students to support, work with, learn from, and grow with one another. Opportunities for these lateral relationships among students are created to leverage and benefit from the synergy of their peers. When you have Extraordinary Connections where cohesion exists, everyone feels a part of a system that benefits them, resources are shared, and these partnerships allow each student to live in their authentic truth while working toward individual or group goals.

I'll never forget working with a group of educators, teaching them the concepts of how this idea of a collective work and responsibility in the classroom looks. I was breaking down exactly what this looks like, how to do this, and some of the benefits it creates—not just for learners but for teachers too. One particular teacher's eyes lit up as we were going through the activities. I thought if they got any bigger she was going to burst! Because she was clearly very excited, I asked what was on her mind. She cheerfully explained how she has structured her learning environment in a similar fashion. She explained how because of this idea of intentional, collective work, it has shifted the student experience and her experience as well. She went on to explain

One of the true super-powers of Extraordinary educators is to position students to connect with one another through Extraordinary Peer Collaboration. This is a purposeful positioning of students to support, work with, learn from, and grow with one another.

that some of the built-in benefits not only position students to overcome challenges by working together, but cause students to hold one another accountable, and often behavior is self/peer corrected to keep the flow of learning intact.

The supervising educator for the building was present during this workshop and chimed in to co-sign as to what this particular educator was saying. As someone who has observed this teacher on countless occasions, she has been able to witness that the peer connections are obvious and make a huge difference. This was an awesome, real-time testament to the benefit of Extraordinary Peer Collaboration and how it can shift teaching and learning.

Making Students the Focus

To establish Extraordinary Peer Collaboration, it is important to understand that intentional, proactive measures are in place. This is a deliberate, upfront investment of time and energy to help students develop positive peer relationships and build a sense of community. Morning meetings and community circles are a fantastic way to work toward this end. However, it is critical that these tactics remain student focused. This means giving students the opportunity to speak, interact, and listen in an emotionally safe atmosphere. The goal is to position them for ownership of these connections, and that cannot happen when the teacher dominates the activities.

Students are positioned to make decisions, reflect on their interactions, discuss ideas and concepts where multiple viewpoints can be present, and even taught how to have difficult conversations. This starts with exposure to and explicit teaching of emotional intelligence skills—teaching students to develop the ability to recognize, understand, and manage their emotions.

Self-awareness requires an individual to pay attention to the physical sensations, thoughts, and tendencies that accompany a particular emotion. This type of awareness also involves the ability to effectively tell how much a particular emotion may impact them by understanding its intensity. When we think about this, often when emotions are discussed, there are descriptors. For example "I was very happy" or "I just felt sad all day long."

Once students understand their emotions, self-management helps them to

1. choose how they will respond to those emotions,

2. think before acting, and

3. demonstrate separation of emotion and logic as much as possible.

This can be critical because often the behaviors that follow emotions, particularly strong emotions, are immediate with no thought given to the consequences or outcomes.

When Extraordinary Peer Connections exist in the classroom, during student-to-student interactions, at the surface it may appear that they are just talking or working together, but these connections among peers give students opportunities to use and refine skills in ways that student-to-adult relationships do not. They are opportunities to develop peer-level interpersonal skills, self-regulation, and appropriate behaviors through modeling and reinforcement. Empowering students with these tools of personal competence strongly positions them not only to have solid, mutually beneficial relationships among their peers, but it also promotes a healthy well-being and positive identity development. In addition, it reinforces their beliefs about their own abilities, which is huge as far as effort.

Encouraging Connections Beyond the Classroom

When students are taught these social skills in the classroom and positioned to work together toward common goals, it brings about a strong sense of community, giving way for a "we" over "me" attitude that increases belonging and connection to the community.

One of the awesome benefits I've witnessed from my own classroom experience is these habits spill over into the hallways, lunchroom, buses, and other social settings. I was very intentional about making sure my students worked well together. I did not tolerate students talking down to one another and made sure I positioned them to work collaboratively so that they had shared goals and a mutual desire to be successful. Students were being equipped to understand themselves and others, offering support both inside and outside of the classroom. This showed up as a worthwhile investment of time over and over again because it minimized and often prevented conflict issues among students.

Current methods of ordinary teaching practices have positioned our students for repeated, long periods of isolated learning. Considering that students spend over half of their waking hours in the school setting, establishing Extraordinary Peer Connections is critical to developing a student's sense of belonging. As Extraordinary educators, we are here to deliberately position our students for optimal levels of success through Extraordinary Peer Collaboration that can drastically improve student outcomes, create positive social learning dynamics, and make pathways to ignite their brains in order to develop the complex skills necessary for the Extraordinary Learning Experiences previously mentioned.

Extraordinary Educator Invitation to Reflect

Take this moment to think about student opportunities to connect with one another through Extraordinary Peer Collaboration:

- How are students being positioned to learn about their emotions in your classroom?
- Do students have consistent opportunities to work together and develop mutually beneficial relationships?
- What can it do for your students to establish and benefit from Extraordinary Peer Collaboration?
- What are the consequences of students experiencing social disconnect in your classroom?

5

Extraordinary Teacher Connections

Extraordinary Teacher Connections are individualized and positive adult-to-student relationships rooted in warmth, rapport, high expectations, and trust.

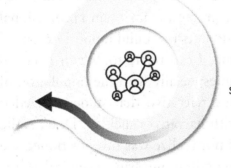

EXTRAORDINARY TEACHER CONNECTIONS

Individualized and positive adult-to-student relationships rooted in warmth, rapport, high expectations, and trust

From the time we are born, we are wired for connection. From the moment you make eye contact with your parents, make gestures and sounds that only a baby would understand, these attempts at interacting and the response given from our parents literally shapes and directly affects the wiring of and development of our brain circuits. These are delicate circuit connections that shape our social, cognitive, and affective processes throughout our lives and lay the groundwork for relationships and connection to become and remain a biological need.

The research shows that children's beliefs about their capabilities are a direct result of their belief that the adults, in this case the teachers, in their life care about them. Meaning that when students feel that their teacher genuinely cares about their well-being and feel supported, seen, valued, and heard, they are more likely to engage at higher levels in learning activities.

The research shows that children's beliefs about their capabilities are a direct result of their belief that the adults, in this case the teachers, in their life care about them.

Unfortunately, relationships are not universally prioritized in classrooms. Ordinary teaching practices allow room for a content-heavy focus, disregarding the need for relationships in the learning environment. These traditional practices give opportunities for educators to create and maintain a professional distance from students, with no effort to build rapport or trust.

Truthfully this is something I can relate to. When I started teaching it was very common, especially with the population of students I served, to push the narrative that students needed strict discipline, supported with narratives such as "Don't smile until November." What I did not realize was this positioned me to be perceived as cold and sometimes uncaring, even if that was not my intent. By not having a deliberate focus on connecting with my students, I facilitated an experience that left my students wondering if I cared about them, if they were good enough, and if they could succeed. In my mind, I was there to teach and get my students to achieve at all costs, not considering that the cost I was willing to pay was too much. It made my job very hard, unrewarding, and emotionally exhausting. Moreover, this persona that I was attempting was not my natural personality.

Connecting Emotionally with Students

Extraordinary Teacher Connections are positive, adult-to-student relationships rooted in warmth, rapport, high expectations, and trust. This is of critical importance, especially for children of color or from underserved communities. The emotional toll of the anxiety that comes with questioning whether or not you belong creates a cognitive load on students that totally undermines any sort of academic achievement.

Extraordinary educators know that students have feelings, insecurities, and reasons why they want or do not want to do certain things in the learning environment. They seek to optimize for feelings and natural motivations as a means of engagement.

> *Extraordinary Teacher Connections are positive, adult-to-student relationships rooted in warmth, rapport, high expectations, and trust.*

As an instructional mechanism that leverages the reality of what drives human behavior, Extraordinary Teacher Connections engage students in ways that help them to understand who they are, what they have the potential to do, and their level of importance to others.

How Is This Done?

Have you ever had a meaningful conversation with someone—someone you needed to talk to, and during that conversation,

Extraordinary educators know that students have feelings, insecurities, and reasons why they want or do not want to do certain things in the learning environment. They seek to optimize for feelings and natural motivations as a means of engagement.

you take the time to break it down, top to bottom, exactly what it is that happened, how it made you feel, and how you're handling the situation? You put a lot of effort into making sure your argument is clear so that the person can see exactly where you're coming from.

But, when that person responds, it leaves you almost baffled. Why? Because it's like the person didn't hear anything you just said. This is because most of us listen with the intent of replying instead of listening for the purpose of understanding. In this instance, it is the listener's habit to filter what you're saying through their own personal experience. With their personal life as a frame of reference for what you have said, their response is prematurely determined before you have even finished. It's as if the communication only happened one way because that person never really truly understood you. This creates frustration, even a bit of resentment, because you end up feeling like you're not being heard and what you say doesn't really matter to the person.

As educators, when we begin the school year, we set out to establish expectations that students are to arrive on time, that homework should be submitted in this basket, or that hats and coats should be hung up before students take their seats. We teach students the rules to communicate—that they should wait to be called on before speaking or that they are to treat others the way they want to be treated. We explain and even demonstrate routines to ensure efficiency and even safety, routines such as how to enter and exit the classroom, fire drill procedures, and how to line up to go to the gym, lunch, and other activities. All of this is so that the classroom can be as productive and safe as possible, right?

But what we have to realize is that this puts us in the position where from day one, we set the tone that communication is one way. We talk to students to convey the rules, the routines, the expectations, the discussions, and the lessons, all instances where we talk to them. And what this does is not allow students the opportunity to effectively talk to us.

What I mean by that is it does not afford us the chance to listen—to listen with empathy with the intent to understand and really get to know our students at their core. Unfortunately, we tend to get into the habit of making sure students understand what it is we need from them first and fully, before we really make an effort, if at all, to understand them. What happens now is we try to teach, manage conflict, and communicate with our students, having little to no understanding of them, little to no understanding of what makes them tick at an identity level. What causes them to spark, what piques their interest, and what do they value?

Extraordinary educators are fantastic at understanding their students *before* they attempt to be understood themselves. What they realize is they are fueling the student-to-teacher connection because students end up feeling seen, valued, and heard. Then, Extraordinary educators use this information to communicate with their students and get better results.

Extraordinary Teacher Connections Versus Extraordinary Peer Collaboration

It is important to note the similarities between Extraordinary Teacher Connections and Extraordinary Peer Collaboration because they both focus on relationships. However, Extraordinary Teacher Connections are a positive adult-to-child relationship, so it is a developmental relationship. It is rooted in adult guidance, positioning students to learn, develop skills, and increase confidence with the hope of eventually releasing them to perform those tasks on their own and be prepared for new challenges. It is a strategic, mutually beneficial relationship that is warm and caring, yet not passive or holding students to lowered expectations. Extraordinary Teacher Connections help lower the barriers, not lower the bar.

Additionally, what's really interesting about Extraordinary Teacher Connections is that this mechanism acts as a form of two-way pedagogy: the students are learning as a result of the teacher, but the teacher is also learning as a result of the students.

Additionally, what's really interesting about Extraordinary Teacher Connections is that this mechanism acts as a form of two-way pedagogy: the students are learning as a result of the teacher, but the teacher is also learning as a result of the students. When teachers intentionally seek to understand before being understood, this facilitates a path for teachers to understand and develop a greater level of cultural awareness. This increased cultural competence, the acknowledgment, respect for, and understanding of cultural backgrounds, helps teachers understand and leverage the obvious as well as the unwritten rules about expectations of behavior and communication. This creates opportunities to help teachers respond and interact in ways that are perceived by students as appropriate, strengthening the student-to-teacher connection.

From a research perspective, relationships, the level at which you connect with others, are a critical component to healthy development and learning. When these relationships are mutually beneficial, culturally affirming, and built on established trust, they prove to be incredible catalysts for high levels of academic achievement for the students.

Extraordinary Educator Invitation to Reflect

Take this moment to think about positive connections to educators through Extraordinary Teacher Connections:

- How have you taken the time to understand your students before being understood?

- In what ways have you demonstrated a focus on rapport and trust?

- How do you leverage positive adult-to-student relationships to hold students to high expectations?

6

Extraordinary Atmosphere

An Extraordinary Atmosphere is a synergistic environment that provides physical as well as emotional safety and elicits hard work while embodying belonging, motivation, enthusiasm, and an authentic love of learning.

EXTRAORDINARY ENVIRONMENTAL CONDITIONS

A synergistic environment that provides physical as well as emotional safety, promoting belonging, motivation, enthusiasm, and an authentic love of learning

I'll never forget the first time my paradigm about traffic lights shifted. Now, while you might immediately think to yourself, "Where is this going, and what the heck does a traffic light have to do with my classroom," let me provide some context.

We see traffic lights every day. All the time. We praise them when we have the privilege of traveling through four or five consecutive green lights, whisking us along our way, and curse them when we're running late and the timing of a red light makes us even later.

What changed my perspective one day was passing by a traffic signal that was down, while construction workers were updating the wiring at a particular intersection. I just happened to pull right up to the intersection, and right outside my window, propped up by a worker on the side of the road, was the traffic light. For some reason, I never considered how large a traffic light actually is up close. It's quite sizable.

The bulbs themselves are typically 12 inches in diameter. To put that into perspective, that's larger than a regulation NBA basketball. For your average red, yellow, and green light, along with the back panels to detract surrounding lights, you're talking about an object that is upward of 4 feet tall. If it's a traffic light with the addition of the yellow and green directional arrows at the bottom, you're talking about a structure that is taller than the average human being.

Besides the fact that this object literally dictates life or death at any intersection at any given time, seeing this traffic light up close made me realize, although this is something that I see quite often, the significance of its size is something that never really occurred to me. It is something I see and interact with every day, but never really pay total attention to in some ways. I believe the same thing happens in our learning environments. Something we see and interact with on a daily basis, but do we really pay attention? Are we really aware of the implications of an ordinary learning atmosphere versus an Extraordinary Atmosphere? Is it even significant at all?

The Effect of Extraordinary Conditions

I'll explain it this way. In the 1970s, Stanford University researchers worked with a group of toddlers to determine what drives their behavior. Separately, each toddler was given a marshmallow and told if they wanted to, they could eat it. However, if they could wait until the person got back, they could have two marshmallows. Eat it now, get one marshmallow; wait to eat it, get two marshmallows.

The purpose of this exercise was to take a look at who could exercise patience, demonstrate impulse control, and delay gratification to earn the reward of having more. Some of the toddlers waited it out to earn the second marshmallow; others did not and only received one. The researchers tracked the toddlers to see if there was a relationship between those who were able to delay gratification and success in school as well as life. Interestingly, the researchers found that the kids who were able to wait had significantly better long-term outcomes. They graduated from high school at higher rates, earned better GPAs, went to and finished college at higher rates, and were considered generally successful.

On all accounts, these children from the age of about 4 to 6 years old, if they were able to delay gratification, predicted their likelihood to be successful. This essentially led to the conclusion that the ability to delay gratification, wait for rewards, and exercise patience was a fixed trait. Some kids had that trait, and some did not. The ones who had it would be successful; the ones who didn't, wouldn't.

This further reinforces the way our system of ordinary education is set up. It makes a lot of sense when you think about how it reflects these very same sentiments. The way it is inherently built, it assumes that some have it and some don't. Some kids will just naturally do better in life than others. This perspective leaves us in a situation where for so long we operate under conditions that some have what it takes and others don't, and we just do the best we can and keep moving forward.

However, more recent research has tested this theory but under different conditions. This time, the researchers wanted to challenge this ordinary idea and see if it really was an innate, impulse-based decision or if something else was contributing to these children's decisions to choose one marshmallow or wait for two. This time, the researchers worked with another group of toddlers, one at a time, but separated into two groups. One group was going to go through a similar test, but under "reliable" conditions; the other group would participate but under "unreliable" conditions.

One at a time, the children in the unreliable group were asked do a fun craft project where they would color. A jar was placed in middle of table out of the children's reach so it would require effort to reach. However, the jar was filled with visibly broken, used, frayed crayons. These children were told if they wait, they would get shiny, brand new crayons to color with. With that information, none of the students made an attempt to use the broken crayons.

When the researchers came back, they did not have any shiny, brand new crayons. They offered their apologies, and the students would begin to color with the broken, used, frayed crayons. A few moments later, the researchers came back with a set of stickers for the children to use for their craft projects. The stickers were very plain and unassuming, but the children were told, similar to before, if they could wait, the researcher would come back with a set of big, glittery stickers they could use instead. Again, because of these unreliable conditions, the researchers came back with apologies because they did not have the stickers. So, the children moved forward using the plain, unassuming stickers with the broken, used, and frayed crayons because the shiny new crayons and shiny stickers were not delivered as promised.

Finally, the researcher came back and offered each child, one at a time, a marshmallow. Similarly to the previous group of children, they were told that they could enjoy one marshmallow now; however, if they waited, they could have two. Almost every one of the children ate the first marshmallow without waiting for the second. The intentionally unreliable conditions created by the researchers offered absolutely no reason for the children to believe that second marshmallow was ever coming.

A second group of children, one at a time, were offered the same brand new crayons and shiny new stickers if they waited. But this time, the new crayons and shiny stickers were delivered as promised. As a result, on average, children in the group that were put in favorable (reliable) conditions demonstrated four times the patience, impulse control, and delayed gratification as opposed to the children in the unfavorable and unreliable conditions. These children made decisions based on the experience they had within the context of what happened around them.

In other words, the context, the conditions, and the atmosphere under which those children were placed determined the traits and characters they were willing to reveal. When we intentionally create an Extraordinary Atmosphere of favorable conditions, we position students to demonstrate traits and characteristics of high achievers.

Extraordinary Educator Invitation to Reflect

Take this moment to think about connections through an Extraordinary Atmosphere:

- How can you encourage the traits and characteristics of high achievers in your learning environment?

- Are the conditions of your learning environment favorable to bringing the best out of your students?

- What can happen if an Extraordinary Atmosphere is not the norm in your classroom?

CHAPTER
7

The End of Ordinary

We end ordinary by creating connection in the learning environment. We tap into what Chloe was able to do with the help of Shane. We know that we have to function inside of a system that was not designed for all students to be successful. And to do this, we must become Extraordinary.

When we intentionally create an Extraordinary Atmosphere of favorable conditions, we position students to demonstrate traits and characteristics of high achievers.

That means a calling that is more fulfilling and allows teachers a greater sense of purpose. And even though I majored in education in college, had an advanced degree in education, and was fully licensed, I was still afraid. I had to learn that I cannot let the fear of change stop any potential I have.

Many of us have experienced, and likely used, some form of ordinary practices in education at some point in our careers. To take such a familiar concept, a place that is comfortable and easy, and request change is difficult. Change as an educator can be intimidating. It can leave you with feelings of angst, uncertainty, and doubt. But I want to encourage you to know that on the other side of that fear are lives that will be forever changed for the better because of you.

I'll never forget one of the most impactful and seemingly obvious yet powerful messages I saw from a fellow educator. The message resonated so well, and connected with so many other educators (and likely noneducators alike), that at the time I am writing these words to you, that message has been heard more than 14 million times. The message, albeit simple, was profound and served as a wake-up call to educators and supporters of educators alike—the message was that "Every kid needs a champion."

Dr. Rita Pierson has been a licensed educator since 1972 and has experience teaching in elementary, junior high, and special education. She has worked as an assistant principal, test coordinator, and counselor. She brought a unique energy to each of these roles—a desire to get to know her pupils, let them know how important they are, and encourage them as they grow.

The cornerstone of her message was "Every child needs a champion." This is someone who believes in them and encourages them to be their best selves. She contends that students, particularly those who come from poor families, often don't receive the same degree of support and motivation as their more wealthy counterparts.

Dr. Pierson wholeheartedly believes educators have the ability to significantly impact the lives of the kids they educate. She contends that teachers should develop intimate, personal bonds with their students and should have a genuine interest in their success and welfare. This type of connection has a profoundly positive impact on children and enables them to successfully navigate the challenges and obstacles education can present.

As someone who believes in authentic connections and the true impact educators can have in student lives, she is of the opinion that educators ought to serve as good examples for their charges. She makes the case that teachers ought to be enthusiastic about what they do and be ready to go above and beyond for the sake of the children they serve. Dr. Pierson thinks that kids are motivated to work hard and achieve at the highest levels when they not only see but *feel* this type of devotion and dedication from their teachers.

To Dr. Pierson, successful teaching requires creativity and innovation, and educators should be open to experimenting with ideas in order to better support their students' learning and development. They should explore opportunities to take

> *Every child, in every city, in every school, needs a champion. Said a different way, every child needs an Extraordinary educator.*

chances and attempt new things in the classroom. Every child needs a champion, she contends, and teachers have the ability to fill that role and have a positive impact on the lives of their students.

Instead of ordinary standards and objectives, Extraordinary educators see an opportunity for Extraordinary Learning Experiences. Instead of disconnected, individualized experiences, Extraordinary educators see an opportunity for Extraordinary Peer Collaboration. Instead of lowering expectations and focusing solely on the content to be taught, Extraordinary educators see an opportunity for Extraordinary Teacher Connections. Instead of an environment of disconnection, oppression, and survival, Extraordinary educators see an opportunity for Extraordinary Atmosphere.

We are defenders of equity. We are disruptors of ordinary. We are everywhere and nowhere at the same time. We are the League of Extraordinary Educators.

Are you ready?

About the Author

Dr. Shaun Woodly is a passionate advocate for education and a driving force for change. As a Hampton University alumnus and a dedicated 15-year veteran educator, he has committed his professional life to cultivating rich, empowering, and transformational learning experiences for students and teachers alike.

His journey in education boasts an impressive array of accomplishments. A decorated K–12 teacher and former university professor, Dr. Woodly has been recognized with numerous honors. Among these accolades are a Teacher of the Year award, a district Inspiration award, and several commendations of distinction that underscore his unwavering commitment to educational excellence.

The architect behind the educator movement "Teach Hustle Inspire," Dr. Woodly has influenced and supported thousands of educators nationwide. He fervently believes that teaching extends beyond the traditional classroom. If you've ever mentored, led, coached, parented, inspired, or motivated someone, Dr. Woodly contends, you are an educator.

Teach Hustle Inspire embodies Dr. Woodly's philosophy of education. TEACH means to "unlock intellectual treasure," HUSTLE means that we "can't stop learning, won't stop learning," and INSPIRE means to "spread love and light."

With an unwavering belief in the power of teaching to change lives, shape futures, and improve the world, Dr. Woodly envisions a reimagined teaching and learning environment. His ultimate goal is to help teachers create engaging, inclusive, and innovative classrooms where every student feels valued, challenged, and inspired. His approach goes beyond improving grades; it's about enhancing lives and fostering a lifelong love for learning.

Dr. Woodly's reputation as a dynamic, engaging, and thought-provoking speaker has made him a sought-after figure in the educational sphere. He consults with schools and districts, motivating educators and providing instructional feedback to improve their practice. His expertise shines particularly in urban and culturally diverse schools, where he supports educators at all levels.

Using current research-based methods in pedagogy, human behavior, the science of learning, and culturally responsive teaching techniques, Dr. Woodly transforms schools and programs into high-performing learning environments. His approach helps reframe the thinking and practice of educators, providing them with specific, measurable, and actionable tools for both immediate and long-term use.

Dr. Woodly continues to inspire and bring about change in the educational landscape, championing the belief that every student can surpass the limitations imposed by traditional education systems. He is not just an educator but a catalyst for transformation in the classroom and beyond.

Dr. Woodly works with schools and organizations preparing educators across the country. His programs are designed to break down the barriers that can limit educator success, allowing them to reach, motivate, and engage all of their students. All meaning *ALL*. These programs facilitate a path for educators to genuinely connect with their students, increasing student achievement and truly transforming the learning environment. Dr. Woodly specializes in speaking and training in urban and culturally diverse schools, supporting educators at all levels:

- Breaking down the barriers that can limit educator success
- Highly engaging, fun, yet thought-provoking messages to inspire guests for action and change
- Transforming schools and programs into high-performing learning environments
- Offering ways to help reframe educators' thinking and giving them specific, measurable, and actionable tools to use in the short and long term
- Offering inspirational stories and practical strategies to not just survive but thrive in some of the most challenging conditions

Please visit our website to learn more:
www.TeachHustleInspire.com

- Speaking
- Consulting
- Professional development
- Coaching
- Merchandise
- Free resources

- Dive into the world of education like never before with the League Educator Professional Development Experience. Going beyond ordinary professional learning, this program focuses on four core areas that foster extraordinary results in the classroom: Extraordinary Learning Experiences, Extraordinary Peer Collaboration, Extraordinary Teacher Connections, and Extraordinary Environmental Conditions. Each area is crafted with a commitment to cultural relevance, equitable outcomes, positive relationships, and emotional safety, fostering a love of learning in every student.

- Engage your students deeply and authentically through culturally significant learning experiences.

- Help students develop mutually beneficial relationships with peers, fostering a collaborative community that elevates teaching and learning.

- Build individualized, positive connections with your students, fostering an environment of trust, high expectations, and rapport.

- Learn to establish a classroom setting that ensures both physical and emotional safety, promoting a sense of belonging, motivation, and an authentic love for learning for each and every student.

PROVEN. RELEVANT. TRANSFORMATIONAL. FUN.

Minimize classroom management issues. Reignite your passion for teaching. Eliminate the burdens of ordinary teaching practices. Learn more at https://teachhustleinspire.com/TheLeague.

Join The League and experience the transformation that comes from being not just a teacher – but an extraordinary educator.

ARE YOU READY?

References

Agarwal, P., & Bain, P. (2019). *Powerful teaching: Unleash the science of learning*. Jossey-Bass.

Berg, J., Cantor, P., Osher, D., Steyer, L., & Rose, T. (2017). *Science of learning and development: A synthesis*. American Institutes for Research. https://www.air.org/sites/default/files/2021-06/Science-of-Learning-and-Development-Synthesis-Osher-January-2017.pdf

Biffle, C. (2018). *Whole brain teaching for challenging kids: Seven steps to teaching heaven*. Author.

Chou, Y. (2014). *Actionable gamification: Beyond points, badges, and leaderboards*. Octalysis Media.

Cashman, K. (2017). *Leadership from the inside out: Becoming a leader for life*. Berrett-Koehler Publishers.

Covey, S. R. (1998). *The 7 habits of highly effective people*. Franklin Covey.

Emdin, C. (2017). *For white folks who teach in the hood. . . and the rest of y'all too: Reality pedagogy and urban education*. Beacon Press.

Gavoni, P., & Weatherly, N. (2019). *Deliberate coaching: A toolbox for accelerating teacher performance*. Learning Sciences International.

Gay, G. (2000). *Culturally responsive teaching: Theory, research, and practice*. Teachers College Press.

Goleman, D. (1994). *Emotional intelligence: Why it can matter more than IQ*. Bantam Books.

Graziano Breuning, L. (2016). *Habits of a happy brain: Retrain your brain to boost serotonin, dopamine, oxytocin, & endorphin levels*. Adams Media.

Hammond, Z. (2015). *Culturally responsive teaching and the brain: Promoting authentic engagement and rigor among culturally and linguistically diverse students*. Corwin.

Johnson, J. W., Johnson, F. F., & Slaughter, R. L. (1995). *The Nguzo Saba and the festival of first fruits: A guide for promoting family, community values and the celebration of Kwanzaa*. Gumbs & Thomas Publishers.

Love, B. (2019). *We want to do more than survive: Abolitionist teaching and the pursuit of educational freedom.* Beacon.

Muhammad, G. (2021). *Cultivating genius: An equity framework for culturally and historically responsive literacy.* Scholastic.

Muniz, J. (2019). *Culturally responsive teaching: A 50 state survey of teaching standards.* https://www.newamerica.org/education-policy/reports/culturally-responsive-teaching/

Nixon, C. (2008). *Learned helplessness* [Video]. https://www.youtube.com/watch?v=gFmFOmprTt0

Oakley, B., Rogowsky, B., & Sejnowski, T. (2021). *Uncommon sense teaching: Practical insights in brain science to help students learn.* Penguin Random House.

Sinek, S. (2009). *Start with why: How great leaders inspire everyone to take action.* Penguin.

Storr, W. (2020). *The science of storytelling: Why stories make us human and how to tell them better.* Abrams Press.

TED. (2013). *Every kid needs a champion | Rita Pierson* [Video]. https://www.youtube.com/watch?v=SFnMTHhKdkw

Willis, J. (2020). *Research-based strategies to ignite student learning: Insights from a neurologist/classroom teacher.* Association for Supervision and Curriculum Development.

Index

in ordinary practices, 92
within us, 82
Neuroscience, 45

O
Ordinary practices:
burden of instruc-
tion in, 72–73
changing, 117–118
in current design of
education system, 70
delayed gratification in,
114
disconnection fueled
by, 71, 92
disregard for
relationships in, 104
and Education Preservation
Alliance, 40–41, 57
ending, 117–119
environment facili-
tated by, 70–71
expectations in, 106–107
expecting different
results from, 24
in fable, 1, 3–6,
13–15, 21–31, 57
isolated learning in, 100
oppressive, 29
results of, 78, 78f
for rewarding stu-
dents, 61–62

student disengagement
with, 90–91
transforming, xv

P
Pace of life, 54–56
Pacing guides, 54
Peer collaboration, *see*
Extraordinary Peer
Collaboration
Perception, of learning
experiences,
75–78, 78f, 79f
Person, Rita, 118–119
Perspective on teaching,
33, 39, 56
Point systems, 61–62, 73
Presence, 54–56
Professional development
experiences, 90
Progress, rewarding, 62–63
Promoting Extraordinary
Connections,
83–84, 84f
Purpose, sense of, 47, 86, 117

R
Recognizing students, 60–63
Relationships, *see* Extraordi-
nary Peer Collabora-
tion; Extraordinary
Teacher Connections